WIRELESS STEP BY STEP

WIRELESS
STEP BY STEP

BY
" DICTRON "

LONDON
GEORGE NEWNES, LIMITED
SOUTHAMPTON STREET, STRAND, W.C.2.

First Published	.	.	September, 1928
Reprinted	.	.	.	November, 1928
Reprinted	.	.	.	December, 1928
Reprinted	.	.	.	September, 1929
Reprinted	.	.	.	November, 1929
Reprinted	.	.	.	February, 1930
Reprinted	.	.	.	September, 1930

Printed in Great Britain by
Wyman & Sons, Ltd., London, Fakenham and Reading.

CONTENTS

INTRODUCTION

THE object of this book is to lead the reader, step by step, to an understanding of such of the principles of radio communication as will enable him to obtain the maximum enjoyment from his receiving apparatus. The basis of the contents is a series of articles published in " World Radio " during 1927-28, which attracted so much appreciative comment that it was decided to produce this book.

A great deal more pleasure may be had from driving a motor-car if the driver is familiar with the mechanical operation of the vehicle and the effect of the controls which allow him to regulate its speed and direction at will. Furthermore, the life and proper running of the car are materially assisted by such knowledge.

Too few people have become sufficiently interested in the elementary principles of wireless to study the chain of events which are incidental to reception. Many are adept and enjoy considerable success in the assembly of their own apparatus ; but how much do they know of the reasons why certain components, joined together with lengths of wire, produce certain results ? Do not anticipate constructional data in this book ; that is not the object. All that is proposed is a plain statement of facts and their application in the simplest possible form.

WIRELESS STEP BY STEP

CHAPTER I

ELEMENTARY FACTS

Early   Discoveries—Electric   Currents—Ohm's   Law–
Electrical   Measurement—Potential   Difference—Direct
and Alternating Currents—Magnetism and Inductance
—Summary of Elementary Facts.

EARLY DISCOVERIES.

HISTORY does not relate the first discovery of the phenomena to which we apply the generic term " electricity." Probably the neolithic man discovered that fur, if rubbed on a dry day, crackled and produced small sparks. The fact that amber when subjected to friction possessed the peculiar property of attracting small objects had probably been known for many centuries before it was first studied by Dr. Gilbert in the reign of Queen Elizabeth. He discovered that this property was not possessed by amber alone, but by various other bodies ; these he described collectively as " Electrics," from the Greek word " Elektron," meaning amber.

The next important development was the discovery that certain bodies—for instance, two pieces of glass— when rubbed with silk repelled one another, and that certain other bodies—for instance, a piece of glass and a piece of sulphur—when rubbed with silk attracted one another. At this period of development of the science generally, there was a marked tendency to regard physical phenomena as being explained by a fluid theory. Thus it was held that heat was a fluid which could be beaten out of metals. It is not surprising, therefore, to find that the attraction and repulsion of " electrics " were explained as being due to two fluids, both without weight or substance which, when equally distributed in a body, neutralised one another, but which could be disturbed and separated by friction, producing what was termed " vitreous " and "resinous " electricity. Over a century ago, this theory gave way to what was termed the " single fluid theory," by which a body was held to contain one form of " electric fluid " more or less evenly distributed throughout its mass. Friction was supposed to disturb the distribution and cause a surplus of fluid in one part of the body and a

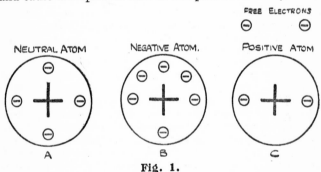

Fig. 1.

deficiency in another, giving rise to the terms " positive " and " negative " (+ and −) electricity, which are in general use to-day, albeit with a somewhat different application. Both hypotheses agree on one important fundamental principle—namely, that opposite forms of electricity attract one another and like forms repel one another. This indisputable fact, handed down to us by the pioneers, is the first and most important step in our study.

We have seen what the early investigators believed and established. What is the modern theory ? We really know no more of the fundamental composition of electricity as a substance than did Dr. Gilbert, or, for that matter, the neolithic man, but we have found out a great deal about what it does and what it can be made to do, and we have evolved a theory called the " Electron Theory of Matter," which if not actually proven, is so closely corroborated by logic as to be sufficiently conclusive to be adopted as a basic scientific principle.

An outline of the principle involved is all that we need consider here. Those who wish to study the subject more closely are recommended to read " Electron Theory of Matter " (Richardson), or " The Electron Theory " (E. Fournier d'Albe) ; in these volumes the theory is treated exhaustively from the scientific aspect.

THE ELECTRON THEORY.

It has long been accepted as a fact that all matter, whether solid, liquid, or gas, is composed of a conglomeration of a vast number of atoms so minute as to be invisible even with the most powerful microscope. But even the infinitesimally small atom has a definite structure and is therefore capable of further dissection. Modern science tells us that an atom of matter consists of a number of even smaller particles called " electrons," which revolve orbitally round a nucleus. All electrons, whatever the matter they come from, are exactly similar in character, and each consists of a minute particle of negative electricity. The nucleus of the atom is identified with what we call positive electricity and will consequently attract electrons. In a normal atom the nucleus will attract just sufficient electrons to neutralise its own positive character. The atom is then said to be neutral and has no charge. If some additional electrons are forced on to the atom, it becomes negatively charged and, conversely, if one or more electrons are removed from the atom it becomes positively charged. Fig. 1A shows a neutral atom, in Fig. 1B two electrons have been added and the atom is negative, while in Fig. 1C we see an atom bereft of two electrons making the atom positive. An electron removed from the sphere of attraction of any atoms is called a " free electron." We can extend this beyond the atom itself to the matter of which it forms a part. Supposing a body consists entirely of neutral atoms, it will itself be neutral. If we remove one electron from one of the atoms forming the body, then the whole body will become positive and *vice versa*.

GENERATING AN ELECTRIC CURRENT.

Now suppose that we remove one electron from every neutral atom in a body and take them out of the sphere of attraction of their nuclei and imprison them in some way so that they cannot escape. If we reintroduce them into the spheres of influence of the now positively charged atoms and liberate them, there will be a concerted rush of electrons or negative electricity back to the positive body which will reassume its neutral character directly all the electrons have once more been gathered into their appropriate atoms. In this process we have caused a flow of electrons to take place, or, in other words, we have generated an electric current. Putting this the other way round, we can say that a flow of electric current may be caused by allowing isolated or "free" electrons to come into the sphere of attraction of a positively charged body.

An electric current can be made to flow by separating electrons from the positive nuclei which attract them, liberating them and allowing them to come into the spheres of attraction again when they will rush back.

We may say, then, that an electric current in its simplest form is an electron in motion To put this in practical application we must be able to control the electron and make it travel in whatever manner we desire. Supposing we had two bodies, one of which was positively charged, that is to say, had fewer electrons than it was capable of attracting, and the other negatively charged or having a surplus of electrons. Now, if we were to bring these two bodies together, the surplus electrons on the negative body would immediately be transferred to the other, and a state of equilibrium would be restored when both bodies were neutral.

Now supposing the two bodies were immovable and were situated some considerable distance apart from one another, we could still restore equilibrium by providing a path along which the electrons could travel from one to the other. Certain substances, such as copper, silver, carbon and iron are more suited to act as paths than others. These are called "conductors."

Since all matter is, as we have already seen, composed of a conglomeration of atoms, it will be obvious that all substances contain electrons, and are therefore in some measure conductors, since they will conform to the ordinary law of attraction and repulsion. No two substances have the same ability to pass an eletric current ; some will pass an appreciable amount, while others under the same conditions will pass so little that it is not observable by any known means. The substances included in this latter category are known as insulators. The following lists show, on the one side materials which are most frequently used as conductors, and on the other side those which form effective insulators :—

CONDUCTORS.	INSULATORS.
Silver.	Dry air.
Copper.	Porcelain.
Gold.	Glass.
Aluminium.	Mica.
Silicium-bronze.	Gums.
Zinc.	Oils, Fats.
Brass.	Waxes.
Nickel.	Indiarubber.
Phoshpor-bronze.	Guttapercha.
Platinum.	Pure water.
Iron.	Silk.
Tin.	Furs and Wools.
Lead.	Cotton.
German silver.	Wood.

Supposing we place a conductor, in the shape of a length

B

of copper wire, so that its two ends touch two oppositely charged bodies separated at some distance from one another ; then an electric current will pass through this conductor from the negative to the positive body for a brief space of time, until equilibrium is restored and the two bodies are neutral again. We have, in other words, passed a current through the conductor. The two bodies and the conductor joining them together are known as an electric circuit, and a current is said to flow in the circut.

In order to maintain a constant flow of current in the circuit, we introduce, in the place of the charged bodies we have considered, what is known as a " cell." The electric cell acts in the manner of a pump, and preserves a constant flow of current round an electrical circuit. It consists of three essential elements, of which two are different types of conductors, and the third an electrolyte or acid solution. In the simplest form of cell a piece of pure zinc and a piece of copper are immersed in a solution of dilute sulphuric acid in such a manner that they do not touch one another and each have a portion of their surface above the solution. The zinc will be found to be positively charged and the copper negatively ; in other words, the zinc element will have fewer electrons than it would nor- mally attract, and the copper element has a surplus of electrons. The purpose of the cell is to maintain this state of separation indefinitely.

If these two plates are joined together outside the cell by a piece of wire, a continuous current will flow from the copper through the wire to the zinc, back again to the cell where the action of " separation " will again take place, and the same cycle of events recur so long as the cell retains its capacity as a separator—in other words, keeps the zinc plate positively charged and the copper plate negatively charged.

The similarity between this state of affairs and that which obtains in the case of a pump supplying water to a circulating system which returns to the well from which the pump originally drew the water, will be readily observed, and is in fact a valuable analogy, since the action of circulating water is very similar to that of a simple electric current.

Let us, then, borrow from this analogy one material fact. The water would not circulate through the system unless some external force were applied to the handle or wheel of the pump which set it in motion. So it is with the electric circuit. No current can flow without the presence of an impelling force. This is termed " Electro Motive Force," or in its usually abbreviated form " E.M.F."

We have already observed that different species of conductors will pass differing amounts of current according to their chemical or physical composition. For instance a piece of copper wire will pass a great deal more current than a piece of carbon under exactly similar conditions. The obvious conclusion is that there is something in the carbon which resists the flow of electric current. This resistance is present in lesser or greater degree in every conductor, and limits the amount of current which can be passed through it.

OHM'S LAW

To summarise the foregoing remarks we find that there are three fundamental properties in any electric circuit, all of which are interdependent—the rate of flow, the E.M.F. at work, and the resistance of the circuit to a flow of current. The rate of flow of the current will depend upon the magnitude of the E.M.F., the effect of which will be limited in its turn by the resistance of the circuit.

In about 1830, Professor George Simon Ohm evolved a " law " from the study of these properties of the electric circuit which has ever since borne his name. This " law " may be said to have laid the foundation of the whole vast structure of science embraced by the term " electricity," and has so stood the test of time as to be still regarded as unassailable. Professor Ohm concluded that if the resistance in a circuit remained constant, then the rate of flow of current in the circuit would be directly proportional to the E.M.F. Put in another way, a current of any prescribed value can be produced by an E.M.F. of a value which is proportional to the resistance of the circuit.

Expressed as a formula, the law is :—

$$E = \frac{C}{R}$$

Where E = Electro Motive Force.
     C = Rate of flow of Current.
     R = Resistance of the Circuit.

This is very valuable knowledge, but has no practical application in this form. It is of little use to know that the price of a commodity is proportionate to its weight. We only know its value proportionately. To know the actual value of the commodity we must be able to say that the price in shillings is proportionate to the weight in pounds, or that the price of the whole quantity is equal to the weight in pounds, multiplied by the price per pound in shillings.

The shilling and the pound are units of measurement, each applicable in its own particular scale of values and in no other sphere whatever. The effect of applying a unit of measurement to a scale other than its own is as meaningless as it would be to say that one had purchased two shillings of sugar at a price of one ounce. Similarly, there must be units of electrical measurement.

We have considered various forms of what may be termed stationary electricity or charged bodies. The first unit to be considered, then, is the unit of electrical quantity. This is called the "coulomb." To say that a certain body is charged with five coulombs of electricity implies something analogous to the statement that a tank contains five gallons of water. We shall not require to refer to the coulomb as a unit, since practically all the matters with which we are concerned relate to move-ment of electricity in various forms. Now we set this charge in motion and a fresh set of units are required to describe the manner and effect of its movements. We have talked of the rate of flow of current. If one were to pass a continuous flow of water through a pipe it would be observed that a greater number of gallons of water passed a certain point in the pipe during one hour than passed during one minute. The passage of electricity along a conductor takes place in a certain time and it, therefore, becomes necessary to take time into account. The unit of current is called the "ampère," and when one coulomb of electricity has passed a certain point in the circuit in one second it is said that a current of one ampère flows. The unit of electro-motive force is the volt. It is analogous to pounds pressure per square inch. The unit of resistance is the ohm.

The unit of electrical power is the "watt," which is exactly parallel to the unit of mechanical power. It will be as well to consider the essential differences between "power" and "work." The amount of work which a man must do to push a wheelbarrow along a level path will depend upon two factors—namely, the force with which he pushes the barrow and the distance he has to push it.

A mechanical engineer says, therefore, that the two factors of work are force and distance, and he has evolved a unit known as the "foot-pound" to express the amount of work done when a force equal to a weight of one pound is exerted through a distance of one foot. A force equal to a weight of half a pound exerted through a distance of two feet is also equal to one foot-pound. Conversely, a force equal to a weight of four pounds exerted through a distance of three inches is equal to one foot-pound. This, then, is the definition of work.

Frequently one hears the same remarks applied to what is known as energy. Energy may be defined as the capacity for work, and can, therefore, only be measured as work either done or capable of being done. The two terms "work" and "energy" may, therefore, be regarded as interchangeable and synonymous. Power, on the other hand, is defined by the engineer as the rate at which work can be accomplished or is accomplished.

A unit was evolved by James Watt, the pioneer of mechanical engineering and the first practical steam engineer, who assessed the power of a horse as being sufficient to accomplish continuously 33,000 foot-pounds of work per minute. This has been taken as a standard and is now universally accepted as the unit of mechanical power called " horse-power."

The relation between power and work should now be clear, and it should be obvious to the reader that there can be no power where there is no work done or to be done. Power is purely an expression of the rate at which work can be or is accomplished. It is simply a matter of observation of such modern conveniences as the tram and the electric railway to realise that work can be done by an electric current. If work can be done, then there must also be power. The work done in an electric circuit is the product of the electro-motive force and the current. Since, as we have already seen, the unit of current (*i.e.*, the ampère) is assessed on a time basis, it is obvious that the power in any electrical circuit can be calculated by multiplying the electro-motive force expressed in volts, by the current expressed in ampères. Thus the current of two ampères at a pressure of five volts represents a power in the circuit of ten watts. The name of this unit of power is not its only association with the unit of mechanical power, since the electrical watt is merely a different-sized unit for expressing precisely the same physical quantity, just in the same way as a pint and a gallon are different-sized units for measuring the same physical quantity.

A watt is 1-746th of a horse-power ; thus we may say that the power represented by a current of 7.46 ampères at a pressure of 100 volts, being 746 watts, is equal to one horse-power.

A multiple of the unit " watt " to which we shall frequently refer in future articles of this series is the " kilowatt," which is the term to express 1,000 watts.

There is also a unit of electrical " work." This is called a " joule " and is equal to the work done in one second by one watt, or may alternatively be expressed as being equal to 0.737 foot-pound.

There are other electrical units with which we shall need to be acquainted in the course of our study, but it will be best to leave the discussion of these until later.

" POTENTIAL DIFFERENCE "

Potential difference is in actual fact a different way of expressing electro-motive force, or, to put it another way, it is a state of affairs which must exist before there can be electro-motive force. In order to understand what is meant by electrical difference of potential, it is neccessary once again to use the analogy of water.

The most elementary student of science is aware of the fact that water will inevitably find its own level. The zero level of water is the sea-level. The hydraulic engineer says that to confine a mass of water 500 feet above sea-level is to establish a " head " of water of 500 feet. From this he can calculate exactly the power which he can extract for his particular purposes. So it is with electricity. The earth corresponds electrically to the sea-level in the case of water, and is said to have a zero " potential." Any body having an electrical charge has thus a potential in respect to earth either positive or negative according to the nature of its charge and proportional to the amount of that charge.

So far we have only considered potential in relation to earth, but precisely the same applies to two charged bodies each having a different potential. Let us consider this again in the terms of the analogy of water.

Consider a house built on a hill 500 feet above sea-level ; the house itself is 30 feet in height and has at the top a cistern filled with water and at ground level a tap. Now, the head of water in the cistern in respect to sea-level is 530 feet, but for the purpose of the occupant of the house, the head of water is only 30 feet ; that is to say, the height between the cistern and the tap which he uses to draw the water. The head of water at the tap, however, is 500 feet in respect to sea-level ; therefore, the head between the cistern and the tap is a quantity of differentiation, or, as we would call it in its electrical parallel, a " potential difference."

Electrically, the same set of phenomena may be two charged bodies, one of which has a positive potential in respect to earth of, say, 20 volts, and the other of 10 volts. The potential difference or " P.D.," as it is generally known in its abbreviated form, between the two is 10 volts. It will be obvious, then, from what we have already learnt of the electric cell, that a potential difference exists between its two terminals. As soon as the terminals of the cell are connected through the conductor to form a circuit the potential difference becomes an electro-motive force.

The potential difference between the two terminals of a cell—that is to say, the electro-motive force which is available to apply to a circuit—depends upon the construction of the cell.

CELLS CONNECTED IN SERIES

Supposing we have two cells, each of two volts, and we connect the negative terminal of one to the positive terminal of the other, the two cells are said to be connected in series and form what is termed a " battery." The outside terminals of the battery will be found to be positive and negative respectively, and if a volt-meter is placed across these two terminals it will be found that the voltage has increased to a figure equal to the sum of the two separate cells, that is to say 4 volts. A battery may consist of any number of cells connected in this manner, and the voltage of the battery will always be equal to the sum of the voltages of the separate cells before connecting them together.

CELLS CONNECTED IN PARALLEL

A cell, or a battery of cells, as we already know, will force current through a circuit. The length of time for which it will continue to do so depends upon its internal construction, in the same way as does the pressure at which it works. After a certain time the voltage of the cell will drop until there is no electromotive force.

Supposing we connect two cells together, not in series

as previously, but with both positive and both negative terminals connected together. It is now said that we have connected the battery in parallel. If a volt meter is placed across the terminals it will be found that the voltage of the two cells is the same as was the voltage of each before connecting them together, but the time for which the battery will continue to force current round a circuit has been increased. This time factor is expressed by what are known as ampère-hours, which means simply that a cell is capable of forcing a current of a given ampèrage round a circuit for a given time.

A cell of 30 ampère hours is capable of forcing a current of 3 ampères round a circuit for ten hours or a current of 1 ampère for 30 hours, the effect of joining two such cells together in parallel would be to enable them to force a current of 6 ampères round a circuit for 10 hours or 1 ampère for 60 hours.

A battery of cells connected in series can be connected in parallel to another battery of cells connected in series. When this is done the cells are said to be connected in series-parallel and both the voltage and the ampère hours have been increased. It is then obvious that a battery of any voltage and capable of forcing current of any magnitude for any length of time required can be constructed by the suitable connection of cells.

DIRECT AND ALTERNATING CURRENTS.

Perhaps the reader is beginning to wonder why this book has been entitled " Wireless Step by Step," since this is the fifth article of the series and the word " wireless " has not even occurred. The writer can only plead for patience and point out that a knowledge and understanding of wireless cannot be obtained without the mastery of certain fundamental principles of electrical engineering. These he has reduced to the barest minimum, but they are essential and must be tolerated a little longer.

So far we have only considered what is termed " direct current," that is to say, the current which flows round a conductor in one direction. Such a circuit is illustrated in Figure 2. B is a battery of cells, S is a switch which can be opened or closed so that current can be stopped and started in the circuit at will. R is a resistance.

The signs used to depict these are the standard conventional signs used by the electrical engineer, and these will be used throughout this book. It is as well, therefore, for the reader to notice carefully the signs used in all cases. He can in this way master the conventional signs without additional study.

Now suppose that we cut the conductor and attach a metal plate to each of the two ends, separating the two plates by a non-conductor or insulator. The circuit is

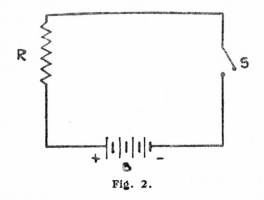

Fig. 2.

now as shown in Figure 3. Even though the switch is closed it might be expected that there will be no flow of current in the circuit, since the conductor has been severed. In point of fact this, under certain circumstances, may not be so. The insulating material between the two plates is termed a " diaelectric." When the switch is closed each plate is connected to one terminal of the battery, there is consequently a potential difference between the two plates. It will be easier to see what takes place when the switch is opened and closed, that is to say, when current in the circuit is caused to flow, if we borrow once more from the water analogy.

Imagine an hydraulic pump forcing water from a well round a level pipe line and returning it again to the well at the same level. When the pump ceases to act, though the pipe is filled with water there will be no flow until the pump is restarted. Imagine that we cut the pipe in such a way that no water is allowed to run out, and cover up one end with a piece of thin indiarubber or other elastic material and then join the two ends together again, we have blocked the pipe, but it is still filled with water on each side of the stricture; it would appear then that no

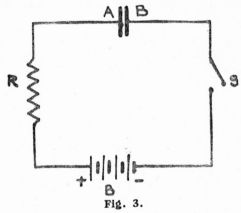

Fig. 3.

water can flow in the pipe line. In point of fact this is not so, because if we suddenly restart the pump there will be a pressure of water on one side of the elastic in the direction in which the water flowed before the stricture was introduced into the pipe. This pressure will cause the elastic material to distend, giving a pulse of pressure to the water on its other side and causing it to flow away from the stricture. Water, then, will flow momentarily in the pipe. The same applies to the electrical circuit, if the switch is suddenly closed the diaelectric will yield, to a certain extent, to the strain imposed by the potential difference between the two plates, and at the instant of closing the switch there will be a momentary movement of electrons along the conductor, and we may say that a current flows in the circuit. The two plates and the diaelectric material, which, in the case under consideration consists of air, form what is somewhat miscalled a " condenser." The origin of this term lies presumably in the fact that the capacity of an electric condenser corresponds to what may be called a hydraulic condenser, permitting a displacement of water. For example, such an hydraulic condenser might be of suitable size to allow of a displacement of, say, one quart for every pound of difference of pressure between its two sides.

Similarly, the " capacity " of a condenser is its power to yield under a given pressure. This is expressed by a unit known as a " Farad." To say that a condenser has a capacity of one farad indicates that if a pressure of one volt is applied to it, it will displace a charge of one coulomb. The condensers which we shall have to consider in relation to wireless communication are of very small capacity, and we shall therefore make use of a subdivision of the farad called the micro-farad, which represents a millionth part of one farad.

Now the condenser is not particularly vital when applied to direct current, but it is of paramount importance when applied to a varying or alternating current. Supposing that by some means it were possible to rotate the battery, Fig. 3, on its own axis in such a way that its positive and negative terminals were alternately joined, each half revolution, to different ends of the conductor, we should pass pulses of current through the circuit every half revolution, each pulse travelling in the opposite direction to the one immediately preceding. The strain on the dialectric is being subjected to a series of pulses, each of which allows a momentary current to pass through the whole circuit, first in one direction, then the other, and a flow of alternating current is maintained past the point at which the conductor has been severed and the plates A and B introduced. Of course, the supposition that the battery is rotated is purely hypothetical and is only used to illustrate in the simplest form a means of generating an alternating current. Much more practicable means are used in reality.

MAGNETISM AND INDUCTION

The ancient Greeks were familiar with a mineral having a peculiar property of attracting iron, or adhering to it with considerable force. They did not apparently discover the most important property of this mineral, its peculiar tendency to turn one of its extremities to the north— that is to say, if a long, straight piece of this mineral were suspended at its centre by a piece of string, it would be found that one extremity pointed to the north and the other to the south. This property of the metal is first recorded in Norway about the end of the eleventh century, and the metal was given the name of " Leidarstein " or guiding stone. The English equivalent which is still in use to-day is " Lodestone."

The stone does not attract metals equally along its whole length, but it exerts the greatest force at its two ends, the north and south poles. Another peculiar property of this stone is its ability to impart its power of attracting metals to other objects. For instance, a bar of hard steel, if stroked with a lodestone, will be possessed of the same powers and will behave in the same manner. A steel bar prepared in this way is termed the " Bar Magnet," and it retains the properties derived from the lodestone indefinitely, provided that it is carefully preserved. It will be found that the bar magnet if allowed to pivot on its centre will always take up a position with its length running north and south. Moreover, the same end will always point north.

Everybody is aware of the properties of the magnet to attract small pieces of metal and similar objects. By a very simple experiment it can be found that the greatest attractive power of a bar magnet lies in its two extremities. If we take a magnet and place it on the table, covering it with a piece of paper, and then sprinkle some fine steel or metal filings on the paper and blow upon the filings gently, it will be found that some are retained on the paper by the force of the magnet acting through the paper, while those outside the sphere of force, or "magnetic field," as it is called, of the magnet will be blown from the paper. Those remaining will be found to have taken up a definite form, having greater density at the two poles than in the centre.

This formation indicates what are termed the magnetic lines of force.

Now if we remove the steel filings and the sheet of paper and arrange a loop of wire just large enough to pass over the section of the bar magnet without touching it, we should find that if we suspended the loop of wire and suddenly inserted the bar magnet inside it, a momentary flow of current would take place in the wire. This is because the wire has cut the lines of force of the magnet, and it is said that we have induced a current in the wire. The greater the rapidity with which the loop of wire is caused to cut the lines of force the greater the amount of current that will flow. This principle is the basis of all electrical generating machinery, dynamos, alternators, etc., which rely for their operation on the rapid revolution of specially arranged coils of wire in the field of a magnet.

Any electrical circuit has certain properties in common with the ordinary magnet. If a loop of wire or other conductor is attached to the two terminals of a battery, current passes through the conductor and lines of magnetic force surround the conductor in the form of concentric circles. The difference between these lines of magnetic force and those of the ordinary bar magnet is that they are uniform in density and depth round the whole circuit. The greater the current passing through the circuit, the greater will be the density of the lines of force.

From the above it should be clear that it is possible to induce a current in a circuit which has no source of electro-motive force from another circuit having such a force. This, of course, is so. If a loop of wire is attached to the terminals of a battery and another loop of wire having no battery, but in place of it a delicate instrument designed to indicate minute flows of electric current by the movement of a pointer over a dial, is held close to it, it will be seen that when the first circuit is closed and the current caused to flow there will be a momentary movement of the instrument in the second circuit, indicating that a current has been caused to flow. If, however, we cause an alternating current to flow in the first circuit instead of a direct current it will be found that the needle of the meter will oscillate, indicating that an alternating current is also flowing in the circuit.

INDUCTANCE

The conductor in the circuit, instead of being in the form of a straight length of wire, may consist of a length of wire in the form of a spiral coil. This coil is termed an inductance. Each turn in the spiral is surrounded by lines of magnetic force which cut the lines surrounding the other turns in the coil ; consequently, a tremendous concentration of lines of force is set up when a current is passed through the circuit.

As we have seen above, a current induced in a circuit always flows in the opposite direction to the current in the circuit from which it was induced. This principle holds good in considering the spiral coil, so that there is another form of interaction between turns in the coil whereby the current flowing in one turn, while inducing a current in others, is itself under the reversing influence of an induced current from other turns. The effect of this is to delay the passage of a current through the coil as a whole. However, once a current has percolated through the coil and overcome the conflicting lines of force, it will continue to flow without interference, but it will also continue to flow for an appreciable time after the current in the whole circuit is switched off. This state of affairs is analogous to a railway truck in the goods yard. A horse is attached to the truck, and after exerting considerable effort starts the truck in motion. After it has once been started relatively little effort is required to maintain it in motion, but should the horse endeavour to stop the truck while in motion, he will be pushed a considerable distance before coming to a standstill.

The unit of electrical inductance is the "Henry." The wireless engineer, however, deals in minute quantities of inductance and employs a division of this unit known as a "Micro-Henry," representing a millionth part of a "Henry."

A SUMMARY

The reader has now had the opportunity to acquire a knowledge of the fundamental facts of electrical engineering which he will require to apply to the study of wireless. These matters have only been dealt with extremely superficially, and it will of course be necessary to amplify certain aspects to these facts in their particular application. Before actually turning to the consideration of wireless itself it will be as well to devote this article to a summary of the more important elementary facts to which we are likely to have to refer in our future studies.

THE ELECTRON THEORY

All matter, solid, liquid, or gas, is composed of minute atoms. An atom of matter consists of a positive nucleus round which a number of even smaller particles of negative electricity, called electrons, revolve orbitally. They are retained in the sphere of the positive nucleus because opposite forms of electricity attract one another.

ELECTRIC CURRENT

In its simplest form an electric current consists of the movement of an electron or a number of electrons. Certain substances known as conductors allow electrons to pass freely along them. Other substances resist the passage of electrons. The latter are termed "resistances." A substance having a resistance so strong as to arrest the

flow of electrons is termed an "insulator." A current
may be made to flow in any conductor provided there is
a source of electromotive force. If a conductor is arranged
so that its two ends are connected to the positive and
negative terminals of a cell a current will flow through the
conductor.

OHM'S LAW

Current flowing in a conductor is measured by Ohm's
Law, expressed in the following formula :—

$$E = \frac{C}{R,}$$

where E is electromotive force, C rate of flow of current,
R resistance of the circuit.

UNITS

The unit of electromotive force is the "volt," which
is analogous to pounds pressure per square inch. The
unit of current is the "ampère," which is analogous to the
flow of water through a pipe in a given time. The unit
of resistance is the "ohm," the unit of power is the "watt,"
which is analogous to foot pounds per second and therefore to horse-power. "Potential Difference" is analogous
to what the hydraulic engineer terms a head of water, and
may be considered as an "electromotive force in repose"
—that is to say, there is a potential difference between
the two terminals of a battery. When these two terminals
are connected to one another through a circuit the potential difference immediately supplies electromotive force.
The unit of capacity is the "farad" or "micro-farad"
representing one millionth of a farad.

SERIES OF PARALLEL CONNECTIONS

Two or more cells are said to be connected in series
when the negative terminal of one is connected to the
positive terminal of the next. They are said to be connected in parallel when all their positive terminals and

c

their negative terminals are respectively connected together.

Cells connected in series will produce a voltage equal to the sums of the voltages of the individual cells. Cells connected in parallel will have the same voltage as each individual cell so connected, but will increase the ampèrehour capacity of the battery.

Resistances connected in series produce a total resistance equal to the sums of the resistances before connecting.

Resistances connected in parallel reduce the total resistance as follows :— $\dfrac{R1 \times R2.}{R1 + R2.}$ Condensers connected in series decrease the total capacity in the following proportions :— $\dfrac{C1 \times C2.}{C1 + C2.}$ Condensers connected in parallel produce a total capacity equal to the sums of capacities of the individual condensers.

DIRECT AND ALTERNATING CURRENT

A steady current flowing from a source of electromotive force round a circuit in one direction is termed " a direct current." A current which flows backwards and forwards in a conductor owing to reversal of the polarity of the source of electromotive force is termed " an alternating current " and is capable of passing current through a circuit interrupted by a condenser. The number of times that an alternating current changes its direction per second is termed its " frequency."

INDUCTION AND INDUCTANCE

Any conductor carrying current has properties similar to those possessed by a magnet—that is to say, it generates lines of magnetic force. In the case of a conductor carrying an electrical current these lines of force are in the form of concentric circles, of which the centre is the conductor. If a loop of wire is passed over a bar magnet in such a manner that it cuts the magnetic lines of force, a current will be induced in the wire ; similarly the lines of force surrounding a conductor carrying current can induce current in another conductor. An induced current flowing in a circuit always flows the opposite direction to that flowing in the circuit from which it was induced. A conductor arranged in the form of a spiral coil is termed an " inductance." Each turn will induce current in neighbouring turns and will be under the influence of the lines of force surrounding these neighbouring turns, so that there is interaction between turns giving rise to delay in the passage of current through the coil as a whole. Once current has percolated through the coil and overcome the conflicting lines of force it will continue to flow without interference, and will also continue to flow for an appreciable time after the current in the whole circuit is switched off.

The unit of inductance is the " Henry " or " Microhenry " representing one millionth part of a Henry. A current flowing in an inductance will induce similar current in another inductance but flowing in the opposite direction.

CHAPTER 11

WAVES AND OSCILLATORY CIRCUITS

*Waves and Wave Motion—Electro-magnetic Waves—
Oscillating Circuits—Radiating Oscillations—Tuning
and Resonance—Reception of Spark Signals.*

WAVES AND WAVE MOTION

THE basic principle of radio communication consists
of the transmission of what are called electro-
magnetic waves. The nature and form of these
waves are similar in many respects to other kinds of waves
such as water, heat, light, sound, etc.

Let us consider, then, wave motion in its simplest form
and later examine its application to electro-magnetic
waves. Wave motion consists of the transmission of a
stress from one point to another in a medium without
permanent displacement of the medium itself.

If, for example, a stone is dropped into the centre of a
pond, a ripple will travel from the point where the stone
was dropped outwards towards the banks of the pond
without any movement of the mass of water in the pond.
What actually takes place is that the water is displaced
at the point where the stone strikes it, causing a depression.
Owing to the incompressibility of water, the only direction
in which the displacement can be effective is upwards,
resulting in a circular bulge round the depression. As
the bulge descends by force of gravity it causes a further
displacement round it and consequently other bulges,
which continue to rise and fall. We may term the highest
point of the bulge the " crest " of a wave and the lowest

point of a depression the " trough." The wave will appear
to move in all directions along the surface of the water
away from the point where the stone was dropped into the
pond and will appear to move with definite velocity.
Actually, no such motion takes place. There is motion, but
it is limited to a very small region immediately surrounding
the positions of equilibrium of the particles of water which
come within the influence of the displacement of each
subsiding crest and rising trough. It is by imparting
motion to one particle after another that the wave is
propagated, each particle remains in practically the same
position after the wave has passed as it occupied before.
A close analysis of the motion of particles of any matter
subjected to wave motion is an extremely complicated
process, and is beyond the scope of this book. The
important fact is that there is practically no movement of
particles, but that the wave itself moves and with a definite
velocity. One more thing of importance is that the greater
the force which causes the original disturbance giving
rise to the propagation of a wave or waves, the greater will
be the distance which the waves will travel through the
medium, whether water, ether, or air.

Sound waves are exactly similar to water waves in their
behaviour. They are, however, air waves, and are caused
by mechanical vibration. Every vibration of the human
diaphragm in speaking a word produces the same effect
in the air as was produced by the stone dropped into the
water. The important difference is that sound waves
are omnidirectional, whereas those in water are confined
to the surface of the water. Sound travels at the rate of
1,100 ft. per second.

So far we have only considered waves which travel in
media, the existence of which we can detect. Electro-
magnetic waves, or wireless waves, as they are called,
in common with various other forms of wave, travel in a
medium which we call " ether." The discovery of certain
scientific phenomena have led to the formulation of a
theory that all matter is permeated by ether, which has no
weight, cannot be seen, felt, or detected in any way. It
is definitely established that all waves in this medium are of

exactly similar character, that they all travel omindirectionally with the same velocity—namely, 300,000,000 metres per second—and that they may be all regarded as consisting of a series of crests or troughs. The only difference between various kinds of ether waves is the rate at which they undulate. This is termed the "frequency," and is expressed in terms of the number of waves generated per second. It is said that the frequency is 50 cycles when 50 waves per second are generated. A "kilocycle" is one thousand cycles per second. The distance from the crest of one wave to the crest of the next is termed the "wavelength."

There are, therefore, three factors which determine the nature of a wave, the speed at which it travels, the frequency with which waves are generated, and the length of each wave. Now, it must be obvious that the third factor is necessarily dependent upon the first and second, since the length of each wave must be determined by the velocity divided by the frequency. Thus, when considering electro-magnetic or wireless waves, the only quantity which is essential is the frequency with which the waves are generated, and the customary use of the term "wavelength" is, in fact, redundant.

Let us suppose that a wireless transmitter delivers waves to the ether at a frequency of 1,000,000 per second. These waves, as we have already seen, travel at the rate of 300,000,000 metres per second, the wavelength is therefore said, though quite unnecessarily so, to be 300 metres. It is largely custom which has led to the use of this term. It would be just as simple to say that a station had a frequency of 1,000,000 cycles as to say that it had a wavelength of 300 metres.

It is the frequency of various types of ether waves which determines their behaviour. For instance, ether waves of a very high frequency, known as X Rays, can, by the use of certain ancillary photographic apparatus, be used to render opaque substances transparent, but it is only a certain and relatively narrow band of frequencies that can be used for this purpose. Similarly, heat waves are confined to a certain band of frequencies. Electro-magnetic or wireless waves occupy the lowest band of frequencies among the ether waves. They normally range between 10,000 and 300 kilocycles per second.

The important points to remember are that electromagnetic waves travel at the constant speed of 300,000,000 metres per second, that the distance which they will travel is dependent upon the amplitude or strength with which they are delivered to the ether, that they travel in every direction from the point of radiation, and that they pass through practically all substances which are not conductors of electricity, but would not permeate a large sheet of copper or other electrical conductor.

ELECTRO-MAGNETIC WAVES

Just as the waves on the pond are caused by disturbances of the surface of the water, so are electro-magnetic waves

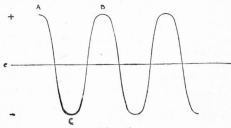

Fig. 4.

caused by disturbances of the magnetic and electrical fields surrounding a conductor.

The simplest and customary form by which this may be illustrated is shown in Fig. 4, which represents the passage of an alternating current in a conductor. The curve from A through C to B is one cycle. The distance from A to B is one " wavelength." If we follow the process we see that during the first half cycle the current is flowing from positive (+) to negative (—); at " C " it changes direction and flows from negative to positive.

If a ball is thrown at a wall, it will bounce back to the point of origin in a direction opposite to that in which it struck the wall. There must therefore be a period when the ball has virtually no movement in either direction. The analogy is not complete—analogies seldom if ever are —but it helps to establish the fact that if the direction of the current in a conductor is subjected to periodic changes, the quantity of current flowing in the conductor must also vary with the changes of direction. The effect of this on the lines of magnetic force (magnetic field) surrounding the conductor will be obvious. We have already learnt that the intensity of the magnetic field depends upon the amount of current passing through the conductor. Therefore as the current varies in quantity so will the magnetic field vary in intensity. In the same way the electrical field—that is the attractive or repulsive field surrounding any charged body—will become alternately positive and negative in character as the conductor becomes alternately charged. That is to say that any charged body within the electrical field of the conductor would be alternately attracted and repelled.

If an alternating current is passed through a conductor it will set up an alternating magnetic field and an alternating electric field all round the conductor. What actually takes place in the conductor is somewhat analogous to the mechanical action of a piece of cord to which impulses of an opposite nature are given alternately. Imagine two men holding the two ends of a piece of cord so that it is stretched, but not tightly, between the two. If the man at one end moves his hand upwards and downwards a wave will travel along the cord. Now, if the man at the other end does precisely the same but waits to impart his impulse to the cord until the other has reached him, a series of ripples, first in one direction, then in the other direction, will result. If this is done very slowly no result will be observable, but if the process is conducted at a high rate of alternations the sound of the rapidly undulating cord may easily be heard. This indicates that the impulses travelling along the string are imparting other impulses to the air surrounding them—in other words, are pro-

ducing a wave motion in the air. This simple analogy
serves to show what must take place in order to distribute
electro-magnetic waves in the ether. Supposing that
a conductor is suspended between two points something
after the manner of the cord between the two men and
an alternating current is caused to travel backwards and
forwards in it, wave motion in the ether is produced, the
ether acting as the carrier of the series of disturbances in
the same way as the air did for the oscillating cord. In
this case, however, the motive force is electrical and not
mechanical as in the case of the cord. Such a conductor
is termed an " aerial " and may consist of a number of
wires suitably arranged.

Now we have seen earlier in this book that all matter
is composed of atoms, consisting in turn of electrons
attached to nuclei. To make the ether (which is the
medium of wave motion) conform to this theory, we must
consider that electro-magnetic waves consist of a series of
disturbances which are superimposed on all the electric
charges in the universe.

Just as in the case of the oscillating cord, electro-magnetic
waves will not be effective for the purpose for which they
are required unless they are caused to undulate at an
appropriately high frequency. The frequencies normally
found to be suitable are between 30 and 100,000 kilocycles
per second. Distribution of electro-magnetic waves in
the ether is generally termed electro-magnetic radiation
or simply " radiation." It is difficult to give an under-
standable explanation of the radiation of electro-magnetic
waves without entering into a long and scientific discussion,
but it is hoped that the foregoing paragraphs have served
to create a correct impression in the mind of the reader as
to what actually takes place. All that it is necessary to
remember is that the alternating currents in the transmitting aerial set up alternating fields around it which
produce a wave motion of the ether similar to that produced on the surface of the water by dropping a stone in
the pond—with this important difference, that the ether
waves move in every direction at the same time instead of
only along the surface of the water. These electro-magnetic

disturbances travel through the ether at the rate of 300,000,000 metres per second, and on coming into contact with a conductor such as a receiving aerial will set up in it alternating currents of an exactly similar nature to those which caused the original wave motion from the transmitting aerial.

For those who wish to examine more fully the scientific aspect of electro-magnetic waves and radiation the following books are recommended :—" Principles of Electric Wave Telegraphy," by Dr. Fleming, and " Principles of Radio Communication," by Prof. J. H. Morecroft.

OSCILLATING CIRCUITS

Electro-magnetic waves when striking a conductor such as the aerial of a receiving station will set up alternating currents of an exactly similar nature to those in the transmitting aerial. They will, of course, vary in strength according to the distance of the receiving aerial from the point of radiation, and according to certain other factors with which we are not immediately concerned.

The band of frequencies used for the radiation of electro-magnetic waves is very much higher than the band to which the human ear will respond. It will, therefore, be necessary to interpose apparatus which will reduce the frequency to a degree which will enable the alternating currents to vibrate the diaphragm of a telephone receiver at a frequency within the range of the human ear. This process we will consider in detail later.

When applied to the process of radiating electro-magnetic waves it is more usual to refer to the alternating currents in the transmitting or receiving aerial as oscillating currents. The terms are of course synonymous in their particular application. The electrical engineer has already appropriated the term " alternating current " for his own particular spheres of activity, the radio engineer is therefore forced by expediency to adopt a separate nomenclature.

The normal method of producing alternating currents employs a machine consisting of specially wound coils which are rotated in the field of a magnet.   There is a mechanical limit to the number of coils which can be rotated in this manner and the speed of rotation.   This limit is very much below that which would be required to produce the oscillating currents required for radiation of electro-magnetic waves.   We must therefore look to other means.

Turn for a moment to Fig. 5.   A and B are two plates of a condenser ; L is an inductance coil and S a piece of apparatus known as a spark gap ; B a battery.   Now there will be a difference of potential across the two plates

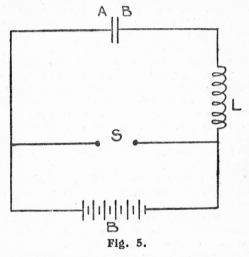

Fig. 5.

of the condenser—that is to say, there will be a tendency for the dielectric of the condenser to break down and current to flow from one plate to another to complete the circuit.   In this condition of strain the condenser is said to be charged.   If, however, an easier path is provided through which the strain can be relieved the condenser may be discharged.   This easier path is provided by the spark gap, which may consist of two metal plates or balls so adjusted that the air gap between them provides an easier breakdown path than the dielectric of the condenser. When the strain imposed by the potential difference across the plates of the condenser is such that the insulation between the two points of the spark gap breaks down, there will be an immediate rush of current from one side of the circuit to the other in the form of a spark across the points of the gap.

While this spark is passing the strain on the condenser is relieved—in other words, is discharged—but the instant after the spark has taken place an exactly similar state of affairs will exist as before only in the reverse direction—that is to say, the condenser will again be charged, the potential difference re-established and the current will try to flow back again. There is no other relief of the strain but a further discharge across the spark gap in the opposite direction to the previous one, so that we have a series of current pulses synchronising with the charging and discharging of the condenser passing through the circuit first in one direction and then in the other. This is an oscillatory circuit in its simplest form.

The first question which will occur to the reader of this book, will be how can the frequency of the oscillations in the circuit be controlled ? It is here that the first fundamental principle of the practical achievement of communication by radiation lies. L in Fig. 5 is an inductance. As we have already seen, there is a delay in the passage of any current through an inductance due to the conflicting lines of force around the turns of wire. This delay will depend upon the number of turns of wire in the coil and the total length of wire in the coil, and will therefore depend to some extent on the diameter of the turns. Put it in another way, and one may say that it depends upon the inductance of the coil expressed in henrys or microhenrys. If we vary the inductance of the coil—that is to say, if we put a greater or fewer number of turns—we vary the time which it would take to overcome the conflicting lines of force and pass a current through the inductance. It is obvious that this variation will produce a similar variation in the number of the discharges of the condenser across the spark gap which may take place in

unit time—perhaps a second, a minute, or another period.
There is another factor which also determines the number
of discharges, namely the actual formation of the condenser
itself. The larger the plates of the condenser the greater
the charge they will accommodate ; consequently the longer
the time to fill them and the longer the time taken to
empty them on each occasion of charging and discharging.
Thus we may also vary the frequency of the oscillations in
the circuit by varying the dimensions of the condenser.
In practice it is usual to arrange that both the inductance
and the capacity of the circuit—that is, the size of the coil
and the condenser—are readily variable to a fine degree.
It is of paramount importance that the required frequency

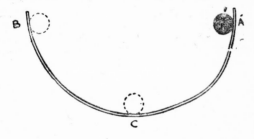

FIG. 6.

should be readily and accurately selected and maintained.

To make quite sure that we have really mastered the
principles of oscillatory circuits, let us introduce an analogy.
Take a piece of cardboard, bend it into the shape shown
in Fig. 6 ; hold it so that it is rigid and cannot rock at the
point C. Now hold a marble at the point A and release
it so that it will roll down the slope from A to C. Having
reached C it will travel up the slope CB through the impetus
which it has gathered. On reaching B, however, it will
not remain there but will roll back again down the slope,
up towards A, down again and up towards B and so forth,
the distance travelled each time being less owing to
frictional losses until finally the marble will come to
rest at C.

Now exactly the same thing will happen in the oscillatory circuit. The condenser having become oppositely charged by the breakdown across the spark gap, almost as great a condition of strain will again exist, so that the same process will again take place in the reverse direction. Just as the marble took shorter and shorter journeys up and down the curved surface of the cardboard owing to frictional resistance, so the flow of current will become less and less owing to the electrical resistance of the conductor. This decreasing backward-and-forward flow of current will continue until a state of equilibrium is established—that is to say, until there is no charge in the condenser, or at any rate until the charge in the condenser is so small and the condition of strain so relieved that the insulation between the points of the spark gap will no longer break down. Then the whole train of events starts once more and continues so long as there is a source of E.M.F. connected in the circuit.

RADIATING OSCILLATIONS

Now let us see how this simple oscillatory circuit fits in with what we have learnt of the radiation of electromagnetic waves. When the condenser is charged—that is to say, before the insulation of the spark gap breaks down—there is an intense electrical strain in the plates of the condenser, in the conductor itself, and in the surrounding ether. There is, therefore, an electrical field which is subjected to this strain. It is simply the case of attraction between two oppositely charged bodies. Now the moment a path is provided across the points of the spark gap a current flows. We have already seen that whenever a current flows in a conductor magnetic lines of force surround the conductor—that is, a magnetic field is created. Current continues to flow until the state of strain is again produced (but it is now in the opposite direction) and the electrical field is again at its maximum, but, so to speak, facing in the opposite direction. It is obvious, then, that during this process of reversal there must have been a point where there was no strain and therefore no electrical field. Similarly, since current flows first in one direction and then in the other, the magnetic field must also vary in intensity and there must be a point where there is actually no magnetic field. It follows that the electrical field is most intense when there is no magnetic field—that is, just before the current starts to flow—and the magnetic field is most intense when there is no electrical field. The intensity of both fields will, of course, decrease as the amount of current flowing backwards and forwards in the circuit decreases.

Now we have already learnt that it is only necessary to produce alternating electrical and magnetic fields around a conductor in order to achieve radiation of electro-magnetic waves. If, then, an oscillatory circuit is arranged to consist of a suitable radiating system and is caused to

FIG. 7.

oscillate in the manner described above at an appropriate frequency, radiation will occur and transmission will be accomplished.

A suitable and simple arrangement is that depicted in Fig. 8 where A is an aerial, which may consist of one or more copper wires arranged between masts of a suitable height from the ground, and E is a metal plate buried in the earth. In this arrangement the aerial and earth become the two plates of the condenser which we saw in Fig. 5 and the process of oscillation is precisely similar. This form of radiation is generally termed " spark transmission " and the form of wave radiated is represented in Fig. 7, which shows in graphic form how the diminishing strengths of the electric and magnetic fields produce a wave which also diminishes in strength. These are termed " damped waves."

Now supposing that the circuit is so arranged that it
has an oscillating frequency of a million cycles per second
and the resistance of the circuit is such that the oscillating
current changes direction one thousand times between
the moment when the insulation of the spark gap first
breaks down and the moment when equilibrium is established, we should transmit one thousand groups, each
consisting of one thousand damped waves per second, but
the waves themselves still have a frequency of one million
cycles. This would be expressed by saying that the

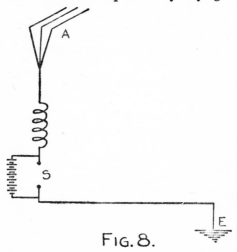

FIG. 8.

radiating frequency of the spark transmitter was one
million cycles and the spark frequency was a thousand
cycles.

We need not give much further consideration to spark
transmission, the writer is happy to say, and many readers
who live in coastal areas and suffer from interference with
broadcast reception by spark transmission will be happy
to hear that it is obsolescent. In a very few years' time
it will probably not be used at all. It has been necessary,
however, to give it consideration in order that we may

master the elementary principles of the radiation of oscillations, and it will be further necessary to examine the manner in which spark signals can be received at a receiving station and heard there in the telephones, because once we have grasped this principle it will be very much easier to progress to our main subject—namely, the transmission and reception of broadcast speech and music.

TUNING AND RESONANCE

In an earlier chapter of this book we studied the conditions under which a current may be induced in one circuit from another. The circuit from which a current

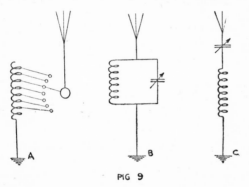

FIG 9

is induced is termed the " primary " circuit, and the one in which the current is induced is termed the " secondary." If the current in the primary is a direct current it will only induce a momentary impulse in the secondary when current starts to flow in the primary, and another momentary impulse when the current ceases. If, however, the current in the primary is an alternating current it will induce a similar alternating current in the secondary, the only difference being that the alternations in the secondary will be travelling in the opposite direction to those in the primary—that is to say, when the current is flowing from

D

positive to negative in the primary it will be flowing from negative to positive in the secondary.

We may say (considering the full cycle of events) the secondary current is 180 degrees out of " phase " with the primary current. It follows that the voltage will also be 180 degrees out of " phase." These considerations of phase relationship in coupled circuits are important in their particular application, which we will consider later. What are more important at this juncture are the principles which govern the amount of current which may be induced in a secondary circuit.

If a current alternates, it must alternate at a definite frequency : there must be a certain number of changes of direction of current in a given time. It is only possible to induce the maximum amount of alternating current in a secondary circuit if it is so arranged as to be suitable to convey alternating current impulses at the particular frequency at which they are flowing in the primary. The factors on which the suitablity of a circuit for any particular frequency will depend are its resistance, inductance, and capacity. Supposing it is desired to pass an alternating current having a frequency of 50 cycles through a primary conductor and induce the maximum amount of current in a secondary, it will be necessary for the three factors mentioned above in combination to produce a natural frequency in the secondary of 50 cycles. Every conductor has a natural frequency of its own, because every conductor has resistance, capacity, and inductance. Perhaps the matter could be more simply understood by an analogy.

Imagine a weight suspended from the end of a length of string and free to swing backwards and forwards. Lift the weight so that the string is horizontal and then release it, the weight will swing backwards and forwards. If the gentlest push is given to the weight each time that it comes back to the position from which it started it may be made to continue to swing indefinitely. It will, however, be necessary to impart each push to the weight at precisely the right moment. It will be found that the number of pushes per minute are absolutely constant, and that if the push is applied a moment too early it will result in a jar to the finger and will completely upset the regular swing of the weight. Now increase the length of the piece of string to which the weight is attached and repeat the swinging process. It will be found that the number of pushes necessary per minute to keep the weight regularly swinging will be less ; shorten, and the number of pushes will be greater. The swinging weight, then, has a definite frequency which depends upon the length of the string from which it swings.

The reader has no doubt at some time or other given a child a swing in the ordinary crude but entertaining apparatus attached to the branch of a tree. Unless the seat of the swing is impelled at precisely the right moment

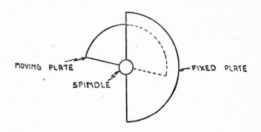

FIG. 10

the effect will be lost and probably the arm will be un-pleasantly jarred.   The same applies to an induced alternating current. If the maximum amount of current is to be passed through a conductor then the conductor must be suitably arranged for the frequency of the alter-nations. Two circuits so arranged are said to be in " resonance," and the particular frequency which they are arranged to carry is termed the " resonant frequency."

For purposes of transmission and reception of wireless messages we may consider the aerial of the transmitting station as a primary circuit and the aerial of the receiving station as a secondary.   If the aerial circuit is so arranged to deliver electro-magnetic waves to the ether at a frequency of, say, a million cycles, then the receiving aerial must be so arranged as to be in resonance at that frequency. The process of bringing one circuit into resonance with another is termed "tuning." This may be done by different combinations of inductance and capacity—that is to say, by altering the size of the condenser in the circuit or by altering the size of the inductance coil. Some of the ordinary arrangements used are shown diagramatically in Fig. 9. " A " is a variable inductance coil arranged so that the total number of effective turns of wire in the coil may be varied by moving the switch to different points of contact. The greater the number of turns in circuit the lower the resonant frequency. " B " is a fixed inductance tuned by a parallel variable condenser. A variable condenser normally consists of one or more fixed plates and one or more movable plates. The two sets of plates are insulated from one another, usually by air, and are so arranged that by rotating a concentric spindle to which the movable plates are attached the area of overlap between the two sets of plates may be varied. The greater the area of overlap the greater the capacity of the condenser (this is illustrated in Fig. 10). It follows that the greater the number of fixed and moving plates the greater will be the maximum capacity of the condenser. The frequency at which the inductance will be in resonance is controlled by the magnitude of the capacity of the condenser in parallel with it. The greater the capacity of the condenser the lower the resonant frequency. " C " is a fixed inductance tuned by a variable condenser in series. The process is the same as in the case of " B," but a band of higher frequencies will be covered by rotating the condenser spindle. If the same inductance is used for both circuits " B " and " C," and if the band of frequencies covered by rotating the condenser spindle through 180 degrees were in circuit " B "—say, 500 to 2,000 kilocycles—the band covered by the arrangement in circuit " C " might be, say, 1,500 to 3,000 kilocycles.

RECEPTION OF SPARK SIGNALS

The Telephone.—Since the first necessity in receiving an intelligible signal is to be able to hear it, let us begin with a study of the requisite piece of apparatus, namely, the telephone receiver. This normally consists of an ordinary electro-magnet and a soft iron diaphragm. Fig. 11 illustrates a single earpiece. M is a U shaped magnet arranged with the poles uppermost. Round each arm of the U is wound a very large number of turns of fine insulated wire. These two coils (c) are joined in series. D is a diaphragm of soft iron which is held in such a position as to be immediately over, but not touching, the two poles of the magnet. In this position the diaphragm is in the most intense electro-magnetic field.

Now if the two ends of the coils are attached to the two terminals of a battery, current will pass through the windings and an intensive magnetic field will be created causing the magnet to exert a pull on the thin iron diaphragm resulting in its distortion to a slightly curved shape. This pull will continue so long as the battery remains in circuit, but as soon as it is disconnected the diaphragm will spring back to its normal position. If the telephone earpiece were applied to the ear and a switch arranged to cut the battery in and out of circuit, the movement of the diaphragm would be heard as a "click" in the telephone each time the switch was closed and opened. If it were possible to open and close the switch a thousand times a second the diaphragm would move backwards and forwards at an equal rate, and the sound produced in the telephone would be a thousand cycle note, which is approximately the same note as the C on the piano two octaves above middle C.

Now supposing instead of connecting the earpiece to a battery we connected it to an aerial circuit similar to that which we have studied in connection with spark transmission, and tuned the aerial circuit to the frequency of a spark transmitter which we wish to hear, say a million cycles (300 metres). We have already learnt that electro-

magnetic waves distributed by the transmitting aerial
produce an alternating current and consequently an
alternating E.M.F. in the receiving aerial similar in
character and in frequency to the alternating current and
E.M.F. which produce waves from the transmitting aerial.
It might be expected that all that was necessary in order
to achieve intelligible communication would be to make
and break the oscillatory circuit of the transmitter in a

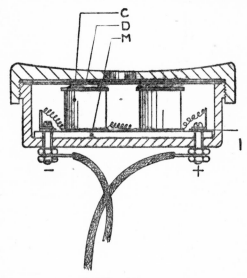

FIG. 11.

series of dots and dashes according to a prearranged code
in order to hear similar dots and dashes in the telephone
of the receiver. But this is not so. Actually all this
arrangement would produce would be a " click " in the
telephone each time the oscillatory circuit was started and
stopped at the transmitter, but nothing at all in between
the starting and stopping process. This is because the
frequency of the oscillations is so high that the iron diaphragm of the telephone is mechanically incapable of

vibrating at that speed. Even if it were possible to devise some alternative mechanical arrangement which would vibrate at the desired frequency it would not be possible to hear the vibrations, because the human ear cannot detect any sound of which the frequency is higher than about 15,000 cycles. There are, however, people

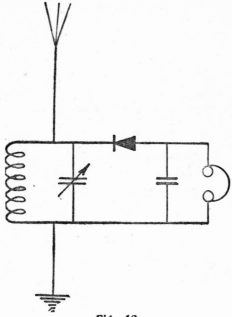

Fig. 12.

with abnormal ears who claim to be able to hear frequencies as high as 25,000, but 15,000 is the normal limit; there are many who cannot hear anything higher than 10,000 cycles. It is therefore necessary to devise some means whereby the action of the oscillations in the transmitting aerial may be interupted intelligibly at a frequency which can be heard.

The Rectifier.—For this purpose we employ what is

usually known as a "detector." Actually this is a misnomer, since the apparatus does not "detect" electro-magnetic waves but enables the human ear to detect the resultant sound. It is more properly called a "rectifier." The term "rectifier" is applied electrically to any apparatus which converts an alternating current into a direct current or pulses of direct current, that is to say, it converts a current travelling first in one direction and then in the other, into a unidirectional current or pulses of unidirectional current. The simplest form of rectifier used to convert the high frequency alternating current produced in a receiving aerial by electro-magnetic waves consists of one of various types of mineral crystals which have the property of affording a low resistance to current passing through them in one direction and a very high resistance amounting almost to a complete stoppage of current in the opposite direction.

Fig. 12 shows the complete circuit consisting of an aerial and earth, tuned inductance, crystal rectifier and telephones. The aerial circuit being tuned to the appro-priate frequency an alternating E.M.F. will exist across the ends of the coil and consequently in the whole circuit. The alternations are at a frequency of a million cycles a second but they can only flow in one direction through the crystal. If the supply of waves from the transmitter were continuous nothing would be heard in the telephones. Consider what would happen. The first half of the first wave travelling say from positive to negative would pass through the crystal and telephone circuit and would cause the magnet to exert a pull on the diaphragm. The next half wave from negative to positive would not pass through the crystal, the first half of the next wave would pass and so on, but the diaphragm which can only vibrate slowly owing to its mechanical limitation does not get a chance to recover because of the very high frequency of the repeated pulls from the magnet and remains permanently bent.

In spark transmission we have to deal with damped waves and as we have already learnt these arrive at the receiving aerial in the form of groups of waves, the number of groups per second being dependent upon the spark frequency, that is, the time taken by the condenser in the oscillatory circuit of the transmitter to discharge through the spark gap.

Now the problem is much simpler. The first half wave of a group arrives in the aerial circuit of the receiver, passes the crystal and the magnet exerts a pull on the telephone diaphragm. The half wave in the opposite direction does not pass the crystal, the first half of the next wave passes and so on until the end of the group is reached. At this point there is, so to speak, a "stand easy" while the condenser in the oscillatory circuit of the transmitter is being charged again preparatory to the next discharge across the spark gap. This gives the diaphragm an opportunity to recover its normal position until the next group comes along and repeats the whole process. A pulse of unidirectional current passes through the coil of the telephone with the arrival of each group of waves. The diaphragm vibrates at the same frequency as the groups of waves, that is to say, the same number of times per second as the insulation of the spark gap in the oscillatory circuit of the transmitter breaks down. If this occurs a thousand times per second, then the diaphragm will vibrate at the frequency and at a note of approximately the same pitch as the C on the piano two octaves above middle C will be heard in the telephone receiver whenever and for so long as the transmitter is put into a state of oscillation. It remains only for the oscillations of the transmitter to be stopped and started in accordance with a prearranged code in order to be able to transmit intelligible messages to the receiver.

The important thing to remember is that waves having a frequency of a million cycles are divided up into groups. The arrival of each group at the receiver aerial causes a fresh pulse of unidirectional current to pass *via* the rectifier through the telephones. The end of the group releases the pull on the diaphragm which recovers its normal position until the next group arrives.

CHAPTER III

THE VALVE

Electron Emission—The 2 Electrode Valve—The 3 Electrode Valve—Valve Characteristics.

ELECTRON EMISSION

WE have now mastered the elementary principles of transmission and reception in their simplest forms, namely, the damped wave system. Before progressing to a study of the use of continuous waves and from that to wireless telephony, it is necessary to digress and undertake a study of the thermionic valve. For this we must go back for a short space almost to the beginning of our studies.

As was outlined in the first chapter, every substance, whether an electrical conductor or an insulator, is composed of atoms of matter. Except when a particle of matter is at absolute zero temperature, the atoms of which it is composed are constantly in a state of agitation and movement. The movement of one atom has no relation to the movement of another, that is to say, they do not move in co-ordinated masses. The electrons in the particle of matter, whether they are actually adhering to an atom or whether they are what are termed " free electrons," are, like the atoms, in a state of perpetual motion.

If a particle of metal is heated to a high temperature there is a marked tendency for the atoms to separate from one another. The higher the temperature the more marked is the tendency. It is really the same thing as the evaporation of water. As in the case of water, evapora-

tion of metals takes place under the influence of intense
heat. Now the process of evaporation consists merely
of a state of separation of atoms which become so violently
agitated that the more rapidly moving ones break right
away from the mass of the metal. It follows then that if
atoms can break away so also can electrons. This is the
basic principle on which the thermionic valve operates.

If a piece of tungsten steel in the form of a very thin
wire is supported in a vacuum tube and heated to in-
candescence, a number of electrons will be emitted from
the wire. It might be thought that quite a large amount
of electrical current could be generated in this way by
heating the tungsten steel to an adequate temperature.
This is not so, because although a relatively large number
of electrons are emitted by the filament, as it is properly
called, into a vacuum surrounding it, they must at once
re-enter the surface from which they were emitted because
there is nothing else in their immediate vicinity to attract
them.

Suppose, however, that a metal plate having a positive
charge is introduced into a vacuum tube and placed close
to the heated filament, there will then be two influences
at work on the emitted electron, one from the filament
attracting it back again and the other from the positively
charged plate. If the potential of the plate or " anode "
is made sufficiently positive in relation to the filament,
the electrons emitted from the heated surface of the latter
will be attracted to the plate and will adhere to it instead
of re-entering the surface of the filament. If there is an
external connection between the plate and the heated
filament, it is obvious that a continuous flow of current
can be maintained through the valve.

The plate and the filament are termed " electrodes."
The filament may consist of one of several metals which
may be coated with various substances having different
effects upon its power to emit electrons at higher or
lower temperatures. The filament is heated electrically
—that is to say, one external connection from the
vacuum tube is attached to the positive terminal of
a battery and the other to the negative terminal. If

a variable resistance is inserted in this filament heating circuit, the extent to which the filament will emit electrons can be controlled by the amount of current which is allowed to pass through it, which is the same thing as saying that it is controlled by the temperature of the metal forming the filament. The greater the temperature the greater the number of electrons emitted, the only limiting factor being the heat which the filament will stand without melting.

The higher the positive potential of the plate the greater the number of electrons which it will attract from the filament. Therefore the greater the flow of current through the whole circuit.

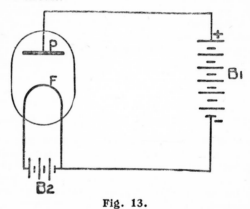

Fig. 13.

There is, however, no object in increasing the plate potential beyond the point at which all the electrons emitted by the filament are being collected and none allowed to fall back again. Obviously, when this occurs the maximum current is passing and no increase of plate potential will add to it. This is called the "saturation current."

If it were so arranged that the difference of potential between the two electrodes were reversed, making the plate negative in respect to the filament, there would be no flow of current in the reverse direction, since the plate would repel the emitted electrons. The valve can only pass current in one direction. This is an important point to remember and we shall be intimately concerned with it in the future when we come to consider the valve as a rectifier of alternating currents.

The valve is shown diagrammatically in Fig. 13. F is the filament, P the plate. The circuit is completed externally through the battery B 1. Battery B 2 is solely concerned with heating the filament to the correct temperature, and it is important to bear in mind that this is its only function. It is not concerned in any way with the action of the valve.

The phenomenon of electron emission in a vacuum was first introduced in 1884 as the property of the Edison lamp. About 1896 the matter was taken up by Fleming, who made an exhaustive study of the passage of current through a vacuum, which enabled him in 1906 to patent a two electrode valve as a detector of damped high frequency waves.

THE TWO ELECTRODE VALVE AS A RECTIFIER

In point of fact it is not a particularly efficient piece of apparatus for this purpose, and the added complications and expense of batteries does not warrant the use of a two electrode valve in place of the crystal as a rectifier of damped waves. In this capacity the valve is obsolete, and it is therefore better to discuss it in a capacity in which it is extremely useful—namely, the conversion of low frequency alternating currents into direct currents. It will be a simple matter for those who are interested to work out for themselves how the valve was used as detector of damped waves, after having seen how it functions as a rectifier of low frequency alternating currents.

The modern use of a two electrode valve to rectify alternating currents is applied in two different ways. The first is termed half-wave rectification. To convert an alternating current to a direct current the valve is connected as shown in Fig. 14. R is a resistance which

represents the load taken by the circuit or apparatus
which it is desired to operate with the direct current
resulting from the process of rectification.

A and B are the terminal points of the secondary winding
of a transformer. We need not stop at this point to discuss
the action of the transformer in detail. It will suffice to
regard it as an ordinary coupled circuit subject to the rules
which we have already learnt governing induction of current
in a secondary from a primary circuit. The primary of
the transformer has its two ends connected to the source
of supply of an alternating current. An alternating
current will therefore be induced in the secondary. A
transformer may be so constructed that the voltage across
the secondary is increased or decreased in relation to that

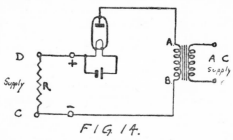

FIG. 14.

across the primary. This difference is approximately
proportional to the difference in the number of turns of
wire of the two coils. Thus, if the secondary has four times
the number of turns of the primary the voltage across the
secondary will be four times greater than the primary.
For the case in point we will consider that the number of
turns on primary and secondary are equal and therefore
that the voltage is equal in both.

Let us assume that we wish to obtain direct current
from an ordinary alternating house lighting supply of,
say, 250 volts of which the frequency of alternation is
50 cycles. During half of the first alternation a positive
voltage increasing from zero to the full 250 volts will be
applied to the point A and consequently to the plate of the
valve, the filament heated by the battery B I is emitting

electrons. As the positive voltage on the plate rises the cloud of electrons emitted by the filament are attracted and current flows in the plate circuit through the primary of the transformer, through the load and back to the filament.

At the next half-wave a negative potential is applied to the plate and consequently no current flows in the circuit because the electrons emitted by the filament are repelled by the negative plate instead of being attracted as they were when it was positive. Thus it will be seen that the first half-wave sent a pulse of unidirectional current round the circuit through the load and back to the filament, the duration of the pulse being half a wave.

At the next alternation, a fiftieth of a second later,

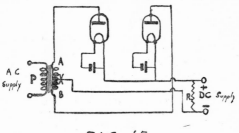

$FIG.$ *15.*

another half-wave pulse of unidirectional current passes through the circuit. We are then rectifying half a wave of each alternation, and the process is termed " half-wave rectification."

The reader may find it difficult to understand why the filament of the rectifying valve is shown in the diagram as the positive terminal of the resultant direct current supply, but if the chain of events is considered carefully it is obvious that a flow of electrons starting from the filament and proceeding *via* the plate, the secondary of the transformer, back through the load to the filamant must leave the point C negative in respect to the point D, which is in fact the same thing as the filament of the valve.

Exactly the same chain of events takes place in the

process of full-wave rectification, except that both halves of the alternation are rectified. To accomplish this it is necessary to make use of two valves and a transformer which has two secondary windings. The circuit is shown diagrammatically in Fig. 15. The two secondary windings may consist of one continuous winding of which the centre point is tapped and a lead taken from it to form the negative terminal of the resultant D.C. supply. Now it is obvious that when an alternating current is induced in the secondary of the transformer the point A will be positive in respect to the centre tap when the point B is negative and *vice versa*. During the first half-wave of an alternation in the secondary A is positive, so therefore is the plate of the first valve, which consequently passes a half-wave pulse of unidirectional current round the circuit and through the load back to its filament exactly as did the half-wave rectifying valve in Fig. 14. During this time the point B is negative ; therefore no current is passing through the second valve. As soon, however, as A becomes negative B becomes positive and so does the plate of the second valve, which now takes up the running, and sends another pulse of unidirectional current passing through the load and back to the filament of the second valve. Thus, each half of the wave is rectified and two pulses of unidirectional current are available at the resultant source of D.C. supply for each alternation.

THE THREE-ELECTRODE VALVE

Having grasped the principle of operation of the two-electrode valve we may now proceed to a study of its latter day development, the three-electrode valve. This study will have to be in greater detail. The three-electrode valve is the keystone of modern radio communication. Without it the transmission of speech and music by wireless would be impossible, and the generation of continuous waves would never have been accomplished. It is not essential to reception, since, as we have already seen, the crystal rectifier can and does fulfil certain requirements, but the valve has very largely replaced the crystal as a rectifier and is absolutely essential for the magnification of received signals in order that they may be heard at great strength in a loud speaker or by a larger number of telephone receivers. The valve may also be used to increase the effective range of a receiver, that is to say, its extreme sensitivity may be used in conjunction with its power of magnification in such a way that signals from far distant stations are rendered audible which would otherwise be beyond the range of the receiving apparatus. Such a fundamental and ubiquitous piece of apparatus must, then, be studied in great detail, but before considering it in any of its applications we must have a thorough knowledge of its characteristics and means of operation.

We have learnt in our study of the two-electrode valve that the amount of current which will flow in the exterior circuit connecting the plate and filament depends upon the heat of the filament and the voltage applied to the plate. This current is usually referred to as the " Anode Current." A curve may be plotted on an ordinary piece of squared paper which will show the variation of " Anode Current " in milliampères corresponding to various filament temperatures, or rather to variation of filament current, since the greater the current passing through the filament the higher will be its temperature. A similar curve may be plotted showing the variation of anode current corresponding to various values of plate voltage. The first curve will show that the filament only emits electrons effectively over a very small range of changes of current, that is to say that the number of electrons emitted is very small when the filament is below a certain temperature. When that temperature is reached the emission rises rapidly, but it will be found that the temperature can only be raised very slightly beyond that point before the maximum temperature which the filament will stand without melting is reached. Something of the same state of affairs will be found to prevail in the case of the second curve. At low plate voltages an almost negligible anode current will be observed. At a certain value of plate voltage, however, the current will be found to increase rapidly, but a very

E

little way beyond this point we shall arrive at the saturation current, that is we reach the point when all the electrons emitted by the filament are being collected by the plate and passed round the exterior circuit back to the filament. The operation of the two-electrode valve, depending as it does on plate voltage and filament current, is, therefore, limited in both respects. These limitations do not affect its use as a rectifier, since the valve may be operated with the filament temperature fixed at an effective value and, provided that a valve of suitable internal construction is used, the alternating voltage applied to the plate is bound to pass through the effective range of plate potential once in every alternation ; in fact the action of rectification depends upon its doing so.

If, however, a third electrode is introduced between filament and plate we shall find a much more useful piece of apparatus ; one, in fact, which is capable of generating, receiving and amplifying oscillation of almost any frequency. This third electrode is generally known as the " Grid," both because of its shape and its action. It may consist of a spiral of wire or a piece of wire gauze, more usually the former. It is placed directly in the path between the filament and the plate which must be travelled by the electrons when the filament is heated and the plate voltage applied in order that anode current may flow. By itself, just placed in the path, the grid will do nothing, but consider what takes place if a potential is applied to the grid. We assume that the valve is operating, the filament is heated, the plate voltage applied and the external circuit closed. If the grid has no potential applied to it there will be no hindrance to the flow of electrons from filament to plate. Now let us apply a potential to the grid so that it is negative in respect to the filament without making any alteration at all to the filament current or plate voltage. What happens ? The electrons find right across their path a negatively charged obstruction ; they are repelled because they are themselves particles of negative electricity and likes repel likes. Consequently the total number of electrons reaching the plate will be reduced, that is to say, there will be a drop in the anode current. The grid being of open mesh, some electrons can still struggle through to the plate, but in much reduced numbers. The more negative we apply to the grid the greater the drop in the anode current. What happens if we reverse the process and apply a positive potential to the grid ? Again, asume that the valve is operating and that the applied plate voltage is fixed at a value which is below that which produces saturation current. This will mean that there are some electrons emitted by the filament which are not reaching the plate and that the anode current is below maximum. Now, if we make the grid slightly positive in respect to the filament the emitted electrons will be attracted towards it. Just on the other side of the grid from the filament is the plate which is much more positive, so the electrons will not remain on the grid but will go on at once to the plate. The grid, being nearer to the filament than the plate, will collect and pass on some of the emitted electrons which the plate has failed to collect, so that the total number of electrons passing from filament to plate is increased, producing a consequent rise in anode current. This, then, is the fundamental principle upon which the three-electrode valve operates, and this is the important thing to remember : the anode current can be increased or decreased by varying the potential of the grid on each side of zero and without making any alterations to the values of filament current and plate potential.

CHARACTERISTICS OF THE THREE-ELECTRODE VALVE

What is of even more importance is the fact that very small changes of grid potential produce very large changes in anode current. A valve might pass say .5 milliampère anode current with no potential on the grid. With as small a negative potential as 4 volts applied to the grid, anode current might be zero, but with about 4 volts positive on the grid the anode current might be about 1.5 milliampère. This is discussed in greater detail un ler the heading of " Amplification Factor."

Of course a great deal will depend on the construction of the wave itself.

For instance, the filament emission is materially affected by the length of the filament, and the size of the plate will make a great difference to its power to attract electrons. These details, however, are for the professional student

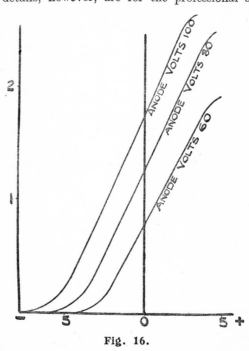

Fig. 16.

and need not be considered in this series. One detail of construction is of importance :—The mesh of the grid. The finer the mesh the more effective a barrier the grid becomes and *vice versâ*. Remember this fact : we shall want to refer to it later when we are considering the application of the principles we are learning now. Certain electrical characteristics must be understood and memorised.

The usual method of expressing the characteristics of a valve is by means of curves showing the effect of various grid voltages on anode current. These are normally termed the " characteristic curves of the valve." Such curves are shown in Fig. 16. One curve is given for each of three different anode voltages. Along the horizontal line the figures represent grid volts on each side of zero ; the vertical line indicates anode current in milliampères.

Nowadays the manufacture of valves is reduced to so fine an art as to ensure almost absolute uniformity according to type, but even so it is useful to know how to plot the characteristic curve of a valve. This is done by connecting the valve as shown in Fig. 17. The only apparatus required

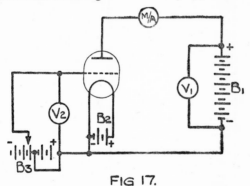

FIG 17.

beyond the anode grid and filament batteries B. 1, 2, and 3 respectively will be two volt meters and a milliameter. A high tension voltmeter V. 1 is connected across the high tension of anode battery, a low tension voltmeter V. 2 is connected across the grid battery, the latter being arranged so that various values may be tapped off. The battery B. 2 is of course only used to light the filament of the valve and plays no other part in the operation.

Now take a piece of squared paper, select a point at which the horizontal and vertical lines are to meet. Mark off equal spaces to the left and right along the horizontal line representing negative and positive grid volts respectively.

Fix the anode battery B. 1 at a suitable voltage and then adjust the grid battery B. 2 until the milliameter M.A. in the plate circuit reads zero—that is to say, until there is no current flowing. This will, of course, necessitate negative grid volts. Examine the voltmeter V. 2 and you will find that it reads say 5 volts negative. Mark off a point on the horizontal line corresponding to this value, readjust the grid battery so that fewer negative volts are applied to the grid, and it will be observed that the milliameter will at once indicate that current is flowing. Mark a dot on the squared paper at a point where the current reading on the milliameter and the negative reading on the grid voltmeter coincide. Repeat the process through zero grid volts until a point is found where the increase of positive grid volts above a certain value produces no rise in anode current. Join up all the resultant dots and you have one characteristic curve of the valve. The process should be repeated with various anode voltages.

IMPEDANCE

Since current passes through the valve there must be resistance in every part of the circuit, even inside the valve itself. The internal resistance of a valve (resistance to alternating current is called impedance) is an important factor in assessing its performance under various conditions.

The impedance of a valve may be calculated approximately by a very simple process. To determine impedance at any plate voltage take a reading of the anode current in milliampères at the point where the curve cuts the zero grid volts line ; this figure multiplied by two and divided into the anode volts multiplied by a thousand gives the approximate impedance.

AMPLIFICATION FACTOR

Another important characteristic of the valve is that which is termed its " amplification factor." We have already seen that small changes of grid volts produce large variations of anode current. Now supposing for a moment that we remove the grid from the valve and leave the filament current unaltered. The only way now in which we can alter the anode current is by increasing or decreasing the voltage on the anode. If we did this we should find that it was necessary to make very large changes in the anode voltage in order to produce the same variations of anode current as we were able to produce when the grid was in the valve by altering the grid volts. For example, we might achieve a change of anode current of two milliampères by altering the grid potential by say five volts. To achieve the same change without a grid in the valve it might be necessary to alter the anode voltage by as much as 200 volts. There is, then, a direct ratio between these two methods which when applied to the three-electrode valve can be related in terms of change in anode volts to change in grid volts. This ratio is termed the " amplification factor of the valve," and can be assessed simply and approximately in the following way.

Select two curves showing the characteristics of a valve at two different anode voltages. Note the grid potential required to make both read the same anode current. The difference between the two grid voltages divided into the difference between the two anode voltages gives the amplification factor of the valve.

THE VALVE AND RESIDUAL GAS

All that we have learnt about the valve presupposes that current flows in it only by virtue of the fact that its electrodes are supported in a vacuum tube. It is impossible completely to evacuate any tube so that it contains no gas at all. There is always some gas present. Even in the most highly evacuated tube there may be several million molecules of gas. Gas being present, there must be electrons in the tube other than those which are freed from the filament in the ordinary operation of the valve. The earlier types of Fleming and De Forest valves were not very effectively or uniformly evacuated. This to a large extent accounted for their undependable and erratic behaviour. The modern process of tube evacuation allows of a fairly uniform degree of vacuum in any number of valves of a particular type, but the amount of residual gas may have a very important effect upon the functioning of the valve.

Normally, gas is a good insulator and will not carry current, but at low pressure, as the residual gas after evacuation of a tube would be, it can be made to carry quite an appreciable current if the atoms of which it (in common with all other substances) is composed can be broken up—that is to say, if the positive nuclei and negative electrons composing each atom can be parted. This breaking up of the gas atom is somewhat similar to the break-down of an insulator subjected to very high voltage. The fact that gas is a good insulator shows that it contains very few free electrons—in other words, there is a high degree of neutrality. In a conductor there are a large number of free electrons or electrodes which can become readily free in the presence of an electric field. But the electrons freed in the conductor are not dislodged ; they only travel along it, which is a very different matter from completely separating an electron from its positive nucleus by overcoming the forces which, as we have already learnt, hold the two together.

This process of dislodgment is called " ionisation," and is normally caused by electrons flowing in the normal stream from filament to anode colliding with those of the atoms of residual gas in the tube with such force as to remove the latter outside the sphere of attraction of their positive nuclei and allowing them to be carried through to the plate as part of the normal stream. The positive nuclei left behind will move in the opposite direction and be attracted by the filament. This will result in a partial neutralisation of the " space charge," so that both actions have the effect of slightly increasing the anode current. This effect may at first sight appear to be desirable because of the increased anode current available. In actual fact, however, there are several serious disadvantages, of which the most important is a reduction in the effective life of the filament, due to its bombardment by positive nuclei. This results in an increase in temperature above that at which the filament is normally designed to emit electrons.

Ionisation is usually caused either by employing too high a plate voltage or too high a filament current, both of which have the effect of increasing the speed of flights of electrons through the valve, thus increasing the force of collision with the atoms of residual gas.

It is obvious that the performance of a valve under conditions where ionisation can take place is entirely different from the normal. Ionisation may generally be observed in a valve in the form of a blue glow, and can usually be stopped immediately by reducing the anode voltage or by reducing the filament current ; thereafter the valve will probably operate quite normally. This applies only to small type receiving valves. In large power transmitting valves ionisation sometimes occurs from a different cause—namely, the overheating of the metal of the anode resulting from too fierce a bombardment of electrons freed from the filament. Certain metals of which valve electrodes are composed contain quite appreciable quantities of gas, which ionisation in the valve itself may free, so that the valve has more gas in it after ionisation than it had before. This, however, is a rare state of affairs and one with which we are not likely to be concerned.

In the process of evacuating it is necessary to ensure that the minimum amount of gas is left in the tube and in the metals composing the electrodes. To pump a glass tube free of the gas contained inside it is a simple process, but metals, oxides, and glass absorb large quantities of gas which they can only be made to give up slowly, so that if the valve were simply evacuated by an ordinary pump it would very soon show signs of containing gas emitted from the glass and the metal electrons. This emission is very slow at ordinary temperatures, and may go on for an appreciable time. It, is therefore, necessary to evacuate the valve at relatively high temperatures, the heating of the glass and metal electrodes allowing gas to be expelled from them very rapidly. This is done by subjecting the valve to a process known as " baking " while it is actually attached to the evacuating pump. The valve must be " baked " at a temperature considerably higher than any at which it is likely to have to operate. It is an exceedingly delicate operation, particularly with valves having coated filaments, since the maximum temperature which the coating will withstand is often considerably lower than the metal of which the filament itself is made. Obviously, it is not possible to heat the tube and the three electrodes in one operation at a temperature which will be the best for evacuating gas from all parts of the valve ; therefore there is bound to be some residual gas.

CHAPTER IV

THE THREE-ELECTRODE VALVE AS AN OSCILLATOR AND RECTIFIER

Continuous Oscillations—Transmission and Reception of Continuous Waves—Rectification—Reaction and Self Oscillation.

CONTINUOUS OSCILLATIONS

WE have now mastered sufficient of the principles of operation of the valve to consider its practical application in various forms. The most important of its many uses is, undoubtedly, its ability to generate and receive continuous oscillations of almost any frequency. If it can produce continuous oscillations these can, of course, be made to produce, in turn, continuous electro-magnetic waves. We have already discussed the process used in the production of damped waves by a spark transmitter relying on the charging and discharging of a condenser through a spark gap in an oscillatory circuit. We found that groups of high frequency waves (the frequency of the waves being dependent upon the tuning of the oscillatory circuit) were radiated, the number of groups per second being dependent upon the adjustment of the spark gap. This method of radiation is effective as a means of communication within certain limits, but it has inherent disadvantages which are not apparent in the use of continuous waves ; that is, waves which are continuous, and of equal amplitude throughout the period of the signal and not broken up into groups of waves of varying amplitude. In the first place a given quantity of power in the form of a continuous wave will pass greater pulses of current through the windings of the telephone receiver than will the same amount of power in the form of groups of damped waves. This is partly due to certain characteristics of receiving apparatus, which will become apparent as we pursue the subject in later instalments, and partly to the fact that the amplitude of continuous waves is constant with each wave, whereas the amplitude of damped waves decreases from the beginning of the group to the end.

Secondly, it is possible to maintain a very much higher degree of constancy of the frequency of continuous waves than of damped waves.

Thirdly, very much less interference from other transmitters is experienced, partly because the oscillatory circuit of both the transmitters and receiver may be tuned more sharply, and partly because the particular process of

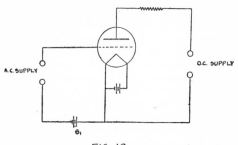

FIG. 18.

reception which is used permits of a variation in the pitch of the note heard in the telephones.

Lastly, a given power may be radiated from an aerial in the form of continuous waves with a lower aerial voltage than would be requisite if radiation were in the form of damped waves.

The action of the three-electrode valve in generating continuous waves depends upon its ability to convert direct current to alternating current. This may seem a somewhat contradictory statement since in our earlier study of the valve we paid a considerable amount of attention to its action in precisely the opposite direction, namely, the rectification of alternating currents with their consequent conversion to direct currents. This only illustrates further the ubiquitous nature of this very valuable piece of apparatus. Supposing that we connected the valve in a manner similar to that in which we have already considered in the explanation of its characteristics, but connected a source of alternating current in the grid circuit. (This is shown diagrammatically in Fig. 18.) Now if the source of alternating current were removed or its terminals short circuited there would be a steady flow of direct current resulting from the electron stream from the filament to plate. The quantity of this current can, as we have already seen, be controlled by the voltage of the grid battery B. The anode may be regarded as the output of the valve. So long as this output is in the form of direct current it is useless to us for the purpose of generating oscillations. We must, therefore, convert the form of this output to that of an alternating current, or pulses of direct current of the required frequency at which we desire to generate oscillations. If we reinsert the supply of A.C. in the grid circuit the process is a simple one. The alternating voltage is superimposed upon the grid Battery B.3. If the voltage variation of the A.C. supply is sufficient it will, in accordance with what we have already learnt regarding the effect of grid volts on anode current, be able to stop and start the flow of steady D.C. anode current synchronously with its own alternations. For instance, at one half cycle the grid is becoming more and more positive and, until at the point where the polarity of the grid voltage is about to change the grid is so positive that the maximum anode current is flowing. During the next half cycle the grid is becoming steadily more negative until at the maximum negative grid volts the grid has effectually barred the passage of electrons from filament to plate. It is here that the value of what we have learnt regarding the mesh of the grid will be immediately apparent.

If an experiment is to be conducted with the apparatus depicted in Fig. 18 it is obviously essential to produce the maximum effect of variation of anode current in synchrony with grid volts, that the valve should have a small mesh

grid. It is also important that the valve should be a
" hard " one, that is to say, one which has been thoroughly
well evacuated, and that it should be operated in such a
manner as to avoid any possibility of Ionisation with its
consequent effect on the characteristics of the valve.

We have then achieved our object—that is to say,
the steady flow of anode direct current has been broken
up under the influence of the alternating grid voltage,
and the output is now an alternating current. We have,
however, only achieved this by the use of external apparatus, namely, a generator of alternating current which we
have used to excite the grid circuit, in order that it may
have its effect on the output of the valve. We have only
assumed the presence of a generator of A.C. in order that a
simple explanation of the process of converting D.C. to
A.C. may be given. In point of fact no such apparatus
is used to generate oscillations with the three electrode
valve because the valve is capable of self excitation without
any outside apparatus.

Apart altogether from the added complication of the
requisite alternating machine, there is another reason why
this method of obtaining an oscillatory anode current is
inadequate. A machine which can generate alternating
currents at a frequency which is high enough to be efficient
for the purpose of radiating electro-magnetic waves
is an extremely difficult and costly piece of apparatus.
The highest practical speed of alternation of such a machine
is in the region of 200,000 cycles, which approximately
equals a wavelength of 1,500 metres. The band of wave-
lengths used for broadcasting in Europe lies between
the limits of 300 to 600 metres or expressed in frequency,
between 1,000,000 and 500,000 cycles—a very much higher
band of frequencies than any which can be produced by a
machine generator. In addition to this frequency limitation, the oscillatory output from such a machine, whether
it were radiated direct or through a valve as already
described, would not be suitable as a means for the convey-
ance of speech and music, but only for messages signalled
in morse or some other code. This method is, in fact,
used for long wave commercial communication in code.

Telephony might be achieved by the use of a quantity of complicated and expensive auxiliary apparatus, but the standard of intelligible reproduction would be very low. Again, a generator of this kind would only give the required performance at the frequency, or very near to it, for which it was designed. All these disadvantages and limitations disappear if the generator is discarded and the valve connected in such a manner as to make use of its ability to excite itself into a state of oscillation.

For this purpose the valve is connected as is shown diagrammatically in Figure 19. L.1 is an inductance coil connected in the anode circuit.   L.2 is an inductance

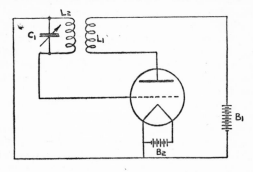

FIG. 19.

coil which may be tuned by the variable condenser C.1. B.1 is the battery supplying the anode voltage in the ordinary way. This need not necessarily be a battery, of course ; it may be any source of direct current supply. We will examine the alternative methods of supply in a later instalment. B.2 is the filament battery. When connection is completed a steady flow of direct current will pass round the circuit of the valve in the ordinary way, that is from the filament to the plate, through the coil L.1, through the source of supply of anode voltage and back to the filament. It might be supposed that some of this current would flow round the grid circuit through the coil L.2. but this is not so, because, as we have

learnt, the line of least resistance is always followed.   The
resistance of the coil L.2 would be considerable.

In earlier chapters we learnt when considering induction
that a direct current flowing in a primary circuit will
induce a momentary pulse of current in a secondary
circuit situated in its magnetic field.   Owing to the " build
up " effect in both the coils L.1 and L.2, the pulse of current
induced in the grid circuit, which we may consider to be
the secondary, will be one of considerable power, sufficient, at
all events, to impress a voltage on the grid of the valve.
The magnitude of this pulse of current may be controlled,
in accordance with what we have learnt regarding tuning
and resonance, if the grid inductance L.2. is tuned by the
variable condenser.

Another thing we learnt when we considered induction
was that the current in a secondary circuit travels in the
opposite direction to that in the primary, and therefore
that the voltages in the two circuits are also of opposite
polarity at any one moment.   If, therefore, we are careful
to connect the coil L.2 the right way round, the induced
pulse of current will impress a negative voltage on the grid.
We have described this pulse of current as having considerable power.   The term, is, of course, relative.   We know
from what we have learnt of valve characteristics that only
a small grid voltage is required to produce large changes
of anode current.   If the circuit is properly adjusted the
momentary negative voltage on the grid will be sufficient
effectually to bar the path of electrons from filament to
anode.   Current ceases to flow in the anode circuit.   There
is, of course, the lag due to the inductance of the two coils,
so that the anode current will die down gradually, but so
will the pulse of current in L.2 and its consequent negative
grid voltage.   When the grid voltage begins to die down,
the grid will become a less effective barrier, and electrons
will once again start to find their way across from filament
to grid.   When the grid voltage reaches zero, there will
again be a rush of current round the anode circuit ; a fresh
build up will start in the coil L.1, and a new pulse of current
will be induced in the coil L.2 ; the grid volts will again
rise to the maximum negative value and anode current

will cease to flow, only to start once more when the grid voltage has died down, and so the process will be continued so long as the circuits remain connected.

The anode current has now been changed from a direct to an alternating one. The valve is, in fact, producing oscillating currents without any outside assistance of a complicated and costly nature. The frequency of the oscillation may be changed at will by a suitable combination of inductance coils and by varying the setting of the condenser. Moreover, the resultant output is of a kind

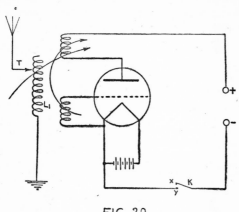

FIG. 20

which is suitable for modulation by speech or music, or is equally suitable for communication of signals in code.

CONTINUOUS WAVES : TRANSMISSION AND RECEPTION

The simplest method of connecting the three-electrode valve to a radiating system is that shown in Fig. 20. Close examination of the circuit will reveal that it is only a slight modification of the circuit (Fig. 19) which we considered as an arrangement whereby the valve could be made to function as a self-excited oscillator. The coil

F

L.1 is the aerial coil, and adjustment of the tapping point **T** will allow the radiating system to be tuned to any desired frequency. This coil is coupled magnetically to the self-oscillating circuit so that the alternating anode current produced by the synchronous variations of grid voltage are transferred to the radiating system.

We already know the effect of alternating currents in an aerial and the resultant disturbances of the electrical and magnetic fields which surround it. We have only to introduce some means by which the whole oscillating system may be made to stop and start at the will of the operator in order to transmit a series of groups of continuous waves, each group continuing for so long as the oscillations are maintained. For this purpose a switch, or " key " as it is generally called, is introduced into the anode voltage supply. When the key (K in the diagram Fig. 20) is closed, oscillation will start and will continue for so long as it is kept closed. When the key is opened, the anode supply will cease and the system will no longer oscillate. The key is generally arranged in such a way that downward pressure of the fingers on an insulated knob brings the two metal contacts, marked **X** and **Y** in the diagram, together and completes the circuit. The key contains a spring which automatically separates the metal contacts as soon as the pressure on the knob is released. Thus, groups of continuous waves, corresponding to the dots and dashes of the morse code, may be delivered to the ether by short and long periods of pressure on the insulated knob of the key. This, then, is transmission of continuous wave telegraphy in its most elementary form.

We need not stay to consider the action of the transmitter in any further detail at this stage. There are a number of alternative methods of connecting the radiating and oscillating systems, but we shall consider these in detail when we come to the study of telephony transmission to which the general principles already referred to are also applicable.

Let us now turn to the reception of continuous waves.

No doubt the reader has been more than a little puzzled as to how signals which arrive at the receiver in the form of continuous waves are to be turned into intelligible sounds in the telephone. When we considered the reception of damped waves we learnt that the diaphragm of a telephone could not vibrate at a high-enough frequency to respond to the oscillating currents in the receiving circuit unless these were split up into groups of damped waves. Now we want to hear continuous waves, and we must resort to another method involving the use of what is termed the heterodyne principle. To understand this principle we must call in the assistance of a piano or some other musical instrument.

In striking a note on the piano we set up vibrations, or oscillations in the air, which impinge upon the delicate mechanism of the ear, thus enabling us to hear the note. The pitch of this note is determined by the frequency at which the vibrations are delivered to the ether. The higher the note in the musical scale the higher the frequency, and conversely, the lower the note on the piano the lower the frequency. Now, if we strike two different notes simultaneously and listen carefully we shall detect a third note, called the heterodyne or beat note, which is produced by the two original notes beating together and creating a third and distinctly separate one. The frequency of this third note is equal to the difference between the frequencies of the two original notes. Thus, if the two original notes struck are middle C, which has a frequency of 256 vibrations per second, and the F immediately above it, which has a frequency of 341 vibrations per second, the frequency of the heterodyne note which they create will be 85 cycles. The further apart the two notes are struck on the piano, the higher will be the frequency of the beat note, and the nearer together the lower will be the frequency. Exactly the same facts apply to wireless, only in a different degree. The continuous waves which we have to hear are of such high frequency as to be beyond the range of the human ear ; they are, therefore, said to be supersonic. Just as was the case with the audible frequencies of the piano oscillations, so it is possible for two supersonic oscillations to beat together and produce a third heterodyne oscillation. This, as in the case of the piano, will have a frequency equal to the difference between the frequencies of the two original oscillations. Thus, it will be readily understood that the heterodyne produced by two supersonic frequencies may or may not be sufficiently low to be audible, according to the difference in frequency between the two supersonic oscillations.

Let us take for example the reception of a distant station which is delivering oscillations to the ether at the rate of 1,000,000 cycles per second. This causes feeble, but exactly similar, oscillations in the receiving aerial. The frequency is too high for the telephone diaphragm,

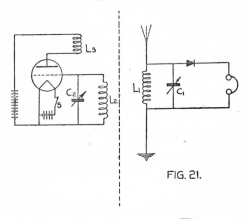

FIG. 21.

so we must change it to a lower one. This we achieve by generating in or near the receiver oscillations having a frequency of, say, 999,900 cycles. These will beat with the incoming oscillations and produce a heterodyne oscillation having a frequency of 100 cycles.

To produce the required change of frequency a means must be found whereby oscillations of a frequency slightly different from those generated at the transmitting station may be produced to beat with the oscillations in the aerial circuit of the receiver. First let us examine the process involved in rendering an ordinary crystal set, such as we discussed in connection with the reception of damped waves, suitable for the reception of continuous waves. Fig. 21 shows the arrangement of the circuits. The two main components, which are separated in the diagram by a dotted line, consist of an ordinary crystal receiver connected to an aerial and earth and a simple three-electrode valve oscillator. In the latter a switch is inserted in the filament battery circuit in order that the oscillator may be stopped and started at will. The frequency of the oscillations in the aerial circuit of the crystal receiver may be brought into resonance with the oscillations radiated by the transmitter by tuning the oscillatory circuit comprised of the coil L.1 and the condenser C.1. The frequency of the oscillations in the valve oscillator circuit is controlled by the setting of the condenser C.2 and by the selection of coils of a suitable size for the grid and anode circuits represented in the diagram by the coils L.2 and L.3.

Now if the switch " S " in the valve oscillator circuit is opened so that the filament is not lighted and, consequently, the circuit not operating, no intelligible sounds will be heard in the telephones of the crystal receiver because the incoming continuous waves, even when rectified by the crystal, will be of much too high a frequency for the diaphragm of the telephone, and even if the diaphragm could respond, the frequency would be far above the audible limit.

If we now close the switch in the valve circuit it will immediately begin to oscillate at the frequency to which the circuit is tuned. If the coil L.3 is arranged in a suitable position in relation to the coil L.1 these oscillations will be transferred into the crystal receiving circuit and superimposed upon the oscillations already in that circuit.

Let us say, for example, that the frequency of the oscillations radiated by the transmitter in the form of continuous waves is 1,000,000 cycles per second and that a suitable combination of the coils L.2, L.3 enables us to generate oscillations in the valve oscillator circuit having a frequency of 1,000,100 cycles. Oscillations of both these frequencies will be present in the crystal receiver circuit, but neither will be audible in the telephones. The two will, however, beat together and produce a third heterodyne oscillation having a frequency of only 100 cycles, which is easily audible. The reader may be tempted to wonder why rectification is necessary at all if, by the relatively simple process of beating two sets of supersonic oscillations together, an oscillation of an audible frequency can be produced.

It must be remembered that the resultant heterodyne oscillation is just as much an alternating current as are the two original oscillations which produced it, and that the diaphragm of the telephone must be actuated by a unidirectional current or pulses of unidirectional current. Moreover, it is the pulses of *rectified* or unidirectional supersonic currents which beat together and produce the required unidirectional currents of an audible frequency. Without rectification we could not pass the requisite pulse of unidirectional current through the windings. The process discussed above may seem to be a somewhat un-necessarily complicated method of obtaining the desired result, and in fact it is so, as there is a very much simpler method which relies on the ability of the three-electrode valve to oscillate and to rectify at the same time. The method described above is, however, the only way in which continuous waves may be received on a crystal receiver.

It may appear to be " putting the cart before the horse " to discuss the use of a three-electrode valve in this capacity before having considered the manner in which it operates as a rectifier of high frequency oscillations, but it is a very definite part of its functions as an oscillator, which is what we are concerned with at the moment. We will therefore assume that the valve rectifies, and defer dis-cussion of its action in this respect to a more appropriate occasion. Turning again to the diagram, let us forget that anything exists to the right of the dotted line—that is to say, let us remove the crystal receiver. In addition let us transfer the aerial and earth, which were part of the crystal receiver, to the two ends of the coil L.2. We have merely transferred the incoming oscillations from the distant transmitting station to the grid circuit of the valve oscillator. We have in no way impaired its efficacy as an oscillator, and there is no reason why it should not continue to oscillate at a frequency slightly different from that of the incoming oscillations. Both the incoming and the local oscillations will be present in the grid coil, and, provided that the assumed rectification is taking place, the resultant beat note would be heard in a telephone receiver connected between the anode of the valve and the positive terminal of the anode battery. This method of receiving continuous waves is generally termed the " self-heterodyne " method.

This concludes our study of the principles underlying the valve as an oscillator and generator of continuous waves. We will now turn our attention to the use of the three electrode valve as a rectifier.

THE THREE-ELECTRODE VALVE AS A RECTIFIER

In an earlier chapter we considered the *two*-electrode valve as a rectifier of alternating currents and remarked, in passing, that it could be used as a rectifier of high-frequency alternations, as, by reason of its ability to pass current in one direction only, it could be used in the same manner as a crystal for this purpose. The results obtained do not, however, justify its general adoption for this purpose, as it is no more efficient than the crystal, and its use involves the addition of high and low tension batteries to the apparatus. The *three*-electrode valve is, however, a very much more efficient rectifier than either the crystal or the two-electrode valve, because it can give not only efficient rectification but amplification of the received signal at the same time.

We learnt in our discussion on the characteristics of the three-electrode valve that the amount of anode current is dependent upon the potential applied to the grid. If, then, we connect a valve as shown in the diagram (Fig. 22) with an alternating generator in the grid circuit, there will be a pulse of unidirectional current in the anode circuit every time the grid becomes positive—that is every half cycle. When the grid is negative, that is during every

remaining half cycle no anode current will flow. But at
the same time we must remember that very small changes
of grid potential produce relatively very much larger
changes of anode current, so that the pulses of unidirectional
anode current are very large in relation to the alterations
which produce them.

If the reader does not immediately understand this
double action of the valve he should refer to page 64
where the matter was discussed fully in principle.

Now let us turn to the practical application of these
principles. There are two alternative methods by which

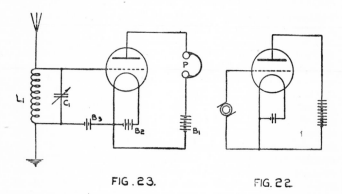

FIG. 23.   FIG. 22.

we may achieve the desired result. The valve may be
made to rectify, either by arranging that variations of grid
voltage produce synchronous pulses of unidirectional
anode current, where none was before, or that an existing
anode current is arrested in synchrony. Let us consider
the first alternative—rectification with increased anode
current.

A valve connected as in Fig. 22 would have to have a
grid of very fine mesh if it were to stop the flow of all the
electrons from filament to anode, even if the maximum
grid potential were of a very high value, so high, in fact,
that when the grid became positive there would be a
flow of current round the grid circuit as well as round

the anode circuit—a state of affairs which would detract considerably from the value of resultant rectified anode current. Thus we see that the circuit as shown in the diagram is purely hypothetical and has served only as an illustration of principle. In practice we shall still need to employ a valve with a grid of a fairly fine mesh, and we can overcome the other difficulty by the very simple process of applying some extra negative potential to the grid. Let us, for a moment, remove the source of alternating current in the grid circuit. There is no potential on the grid and the valve is in every respect similar to a two-electrode valve. When the filament is lighted and anode volts supplied, anode current will flow. Now let us insert a battery of ordinary small dry cells in the grid circuit and so adjust it that just sufficient negative potential is applied to the grid to arrest the flow of anode current. Now put the source of alternating current back again in series with the grid battery and set it in motion. During the negative half cycle the grid is made still more negative, but as we have already made it just negative enough to stop the flow of anode current, no effect will be apparent : it is analogous to a see-saw ; once one end is on the ground, ten additional people can sit on that end without fear of its going any further down. During the positive half cycle, however, the grid potential is raised to a point which allows anode current to flow once more. Therefore, a pulse of unidirectional anode current flows with every positive half cycle where no current flowed before—rectification with increased anode current. This method of rectification is generally referred to as " bottom bend rectification " by reason of the fact that the valve is operating on the bottom bend of its characteristic curve, on account of the extra negative potential which is applied to the grid.

Now let us dispense altogether with the alternator, which has shown us how the valve rectifies and amplifies, and let us replace it with a tuned inductance to which is attached an aerial and earth system. Such an arrangement is shown in Fig. 23. Suppose we wish to receive damped waves from a spark transmitter having a frequency of 1,000 kilocycles (1,000,000 cycles), which is the same thing as 300 metres if we choose to express it in terms of wavelength.

Groups of damped waves are setting up similar groups of alternating currents in the aerial. The coil L.1 being tuned to resonance by the condenser C.1, these alternating currents, extremely small as they are, produce alternating voltages on the grid of the valve. The grid battery B.3 is adjusted so that before the arrival of a group no anode current can flow. If the first half cycle impressed on the grid is negative, still no current will flow, but the following positive half cycle, half a millionth of a second later, will allow a pulse of unidirectional current to flow round the anode circuit, and consequently through the windings of the telephone receiver " P." One millionth of a second later another pulse will flow with the next application of positive potential to the grid, and so on until the end of the group is reached. The cumulative effect of these groups of pulses will cause the diaphragm of the telephone receiver to vibrate at the same frequency as the frequency of the spark discharge at the transmitter, exactly in the same way as did the crystal receiver which we have already studied.

Now let us turn our attention to the alternative method of rectification which relies for its action on decreases in an existing anode current. Before proceeding to a detailed examination it is necessary to reiterate one very important principle.

We have got to produce pulses of current flowing in one direction which recur at a frequency which is sufficiently low to be within the range of audibility. Now the original source of supply, namely, the oscillations generated at the distant transmitter, must, in order to be radiated, have a frequency which is very much higher than any which is audible to the human ear. Rectifying apparatus must therefore be capable of passing pulses of low frequency current through the telephones when the device itself is operated by high frequency currents. We must remember (when considering reception of damped waves from a spark transmitter) that the frequency of the low frequency pulses flowing through the telephone receivers is deter-

mined by the number of groups of damped waves arriving
at the receiver per second, and that the resultant vibrations
of the diaphragm of the telephone are only made possible
by the cumulative effect of a number of unidirectional
pulses composing a group. Each pulse corresponds to the
arrival of half of one complete high frequency wave.
We have seen how the arrival of a positive half wave at
the grid of a three-electrode valve operating as a " bottom
bend detector " allows current to flow through the valve
and consequently through the telephones in the anode

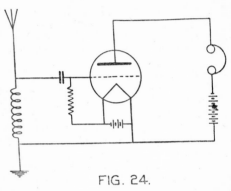

FIG. 24.

circuit, and how the cumulative effect of these pulses
causes the diaphragm to vibrate at an audible frequency.

We may say then that we have produced the effect
required, namely, the passage of unidirectional pulses of
low frequency currents through the telephone receiver,
as an effect of the actual process of rectification. In the
alternative method which we are about to consider the
opposite is the case, since pulses of rectified anode current
are only rendered possible in this method by the cumulative
effect of the arrival of a complete group of damped waves
at the grid of the valve. For this reason the method of
rectification which we are about to discuss is termed
" Cumulative Grid Rectification."

The valve is connected as shown in Fig. 24. The main

elements of the circuit are the same as those which we considered with bottom bend rectification in Fig. 23, but there are the following important differences :—

1. There is no provision for auxiliary grid potential.

2. The grid is insulated from other parts of the circuit by a condenser.

3. A resistance is connected between the grid and the filament.

In considering bottom bend rectification we were only concerned with the current which passed through the valve from filament to anode, and with the effect of the grid thereon, but since the grid is directly in the path between filament and anode there must be a current from filament to grid also. In theory the whole of the electron emission from the filament passes to the plate. In actual fact there are a certain number of electrons which collect on the grid and find their way back to the filament round the grid circuit. In bottom bend rectification this flow of electrons round the grid circuit is so small as to be practically negligible, but if we insulate the grid from the filament, there is no path by which electrons accumulated on the grid can find their way by a direct current path to the filament. So we will provide a path for them through the resistance, but it will be a very slow path and the electrons accumulated on the grid will be delayed there for an appreciable time before they can find their way back to the filament. Before the arrival of any oscillations in the aerial circuit, the valve having a lighted filament and an applied anode voltage will cause a steady flow of direct current round the anode circuit. There is no negative applied to the grid, consequently there is no obstruction to the flow of current. Note that this is the exact opposite to the case of the bottom bend rectification where, by the application of negative to the grid, we arrested the flow of any anode current before the arrival of oscillations in the aerial circuit.

Oscillations are received in the aerial circuit which is

tuned to the appropriate frequency. The grid condenser does not obstruct alternating currents, as we learnt in our earlier studies ; therefore variations of grid volts are applied exactly in the same manner as was the case of bottom bend rectification.

Suppose that the first half cycle is positive, the grid becomes positive and collects a certain number of electrons. These cannot immediately find their way back to the filament because the condenser blocks their way through the relatively low resistance circuit and they are forced to struggle through the high resistance. This takes them a considerable time. Then comes the negative half cycle which makes the grid still more negative and anode current is arrested. As each positive half cycle arrives at the grid more and more electrons are collected. As the crowd increases it begins to neutralise the incoming positive grid potential. The effect of this will be to produce a steady decrease of anode current so long as the variations of grid potential continues. At the end of the group of waves there will be an interval before the next group arrives during which the accumulated electrons on the grid will have time to leak a way through the resistance, thus restoring the whole system to its normal state ready to deal similarly with the next group.

The effect of cumulative grid rectification, then, is in response to the negative half cycle of each wave which arrests the existing flow of anode current leaving unidirectional pulses during the positive half cycles. But these unidirectional pulses of current are themselves steadily decreasing in response to the accumulation of electrons on the grid in synchrony with the arrival of each group. The efficiency of a device of this nature will depend upon the selection of a " grid leak " as the resistance is called, of appropriate value to determine the time factor of the leak away between groups and the choice of a grid condenser which will offer the lowest possible reactance to the passage of incoming oscillations.

REACTION AND SELF-OSCILLATION IN THE RECEIVER

There cannot be one among the readers of this book who has not heard the appeals which all too often have to be made from broadcasting stations against the appalling nuisance of oscillation. Many offenders do not even know that they are guilty, and there must be many who do not know whether they are or not and live in dread of being accused, when, quite likely, their sets are incapable of oscillating. Reaction is the term applied to a state of affairs which we have already discussed in a different

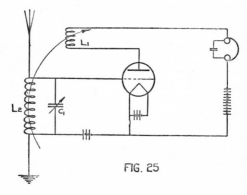

FIG. 25

connection—namely, the effect of the coil connected in the anode circuit on that in the grid circuit of a three-electrode valve arranged to function as a generator of continuous oscillations. We found that if these two coils were coupled closely together, the valve could be maintained in a state of continuous oscillation because of the voltage variations induced in the grid coil, as a result of the pulses of current in the anode coil. In other words, there is interaction between the two circuits, and the feed back from the anode to the grid circuit reacts upon itself because it induces grid voltage variations which decrease and increase the current flowing in it.

Now this reactive state of affairs may be present without actually producing oscillation. Suppose we set a valve oscillating in the manner with which we are familiar and then gradually reduce the coupling between the anode and grid coils, there will come a time when the effect of the reaction is so feeble as to fail to produce voltage variation of the grid of sufficient magnitude to affect the flow of electrons from grid to anode. It is obvious that the valve will at once stop oscillating and will merely pass a steady direct current round the anode circuit. It must not, however, be supposed that because the effect is not observable the cause is removed. The grid is still receiving voltage variations, but they are too small to maintain oscillation, that is all. Now suppose we connect a source of alternating E.M.F. in the grid circuit, leaving the coupling between grid and anode coils at a point where oscillation is not possible. Such an arrangement is shown diagramatically in Fig. 25. The source of alternating E.M.F. is, of course, the aerial circuit tuned to the frequency of a station from which it is desired to receive signals. The voltage variations on the grid produce synchronous variations of anode current, but there is still magnetic coupling between the anode coil (L1) and the grid coil (L2), albeit not enough to create and maintain a state of oscillation. The coupling, if properly adjusted, is, however, sufficient to ensure that the variations of anode current are fed back into the grid circuit where they may considerably increase the strength of the original oscillations in the aerial circuit. It will be noticed that the circuit is arranged so that rectification takes place at the same time. It will perhaps be easier for the reader to understand what takes place if he remembers that everything electrical takes place, virtually, instantaneously, whereas, and in order that the various uses of the valve may be thoroughly understood, we have referred to the processes involved in a way which indicates a relatively slow sequence of events.

Properly and judiciously used then, the process of reaction may be turned to very great advantage in the reception of wireless signals, since it allows of even greater amplification of the incoming signal than that which is inherent in the valve itself. In fact, variations of anode current by reacting upon and increasing the variations of grid voltage automatically increase the amplification which takes place within the valve. Put it another way and say that the amplification in the valve is 10, and if the grid volts are 2 the result is 20, but if the effect of reaction is to treble the grid volts then the total result is 60 instead of 20. These figures are, of course, purely hypothetical. A further effect of reaction is to reduce the resistance of the tuned aerial circuit rendering it more selective and less prone to the reception of unwanted signals at the same time as the wanted one. Now, supposing we carry this reaction business too far, in our efforts to obtain the maximum effect from the feed back of energy from anode to grid circuit, by coupling the coils more tightly together, the result will be that the system will burst into oscillation, and the receiver will be converted immediately into a miniature transmitter which is capable of causing interference with the reception of other receiving stations over a wide area. More will be said on this matter of interference to other receivers in a later chapter, and in connection with the reception of broadcast radio telephony where its danger is greater and its effect more terrible than in the reception of other systems. It is sufficient at this stage to have mastered the principles of reaction, and its close connection with a state of oscillation.

We may now revert for a moment to a matter which we have considered previously, namely, the reception of continuous waves. Here we deliberately make the receiver oscillate in order that we may produce the heterodyne or beat note which after rectification is audible in the telephone receiver. Suppose the frequency of the continuous wave transmitter is 1,000,000 cycles it is only necessary (provided, of course, that coils of the correct size are used) to couple L1 and L2 closely together, so that the set oscillates, and then to set the frequency of the oscillations by tuning the condenser C1 to, say, 1,001,000 cycles to hear a 1,000 cycle note in the telephones. The note may be changed to any more convenient one by increasing or decreasing the frequency of the oscillations. Slight alterations of the coupling between L1 and L2 will also vary the note. This is due to the variation in the capacity which exists between the turns of wire in the one coil and the other.

CHAPTER V

THE VALVE AS A HIGH FREQUENCY AMPLIFIER

Voltage Variation—Alternative Methods of High Frequency
Amplification—Stabilising the High Frequency Ampli-
fier—The Screened Grid Valve.

WE have already considered what is termed the
voltage amplification factor of the valve and
observed the manner in which amplification
may take place at the same time as rectification. Now
let us consider how we may use other valves in addition
to the rectifier in order to increase the signal still further.

Let us forget for a time all that we have learnt concern-
ing the rectifying action of a valve and consider a circuit
such as that in Fig. 26. Note that there is no provision of
auxiliary grid potential or grid leak and condenser, in
fact none of the aids to rectification are present. Suppose
we use a valve having a fairly open mesh grid, that is
to say that when it is negative it is not a particularly
effective barrier against the flow of electrons from filament
to anode. The aerial circuit is tuned to the oscillations of
a distant transmitter producing variations of grid voltage.
If the circuit is correctly arranged and the characteristics
of the valve are correct, then a state of affairs may exist
where the positive swing of the grid may, if it is not too
large, produce as much increase of anode current as the
negative produces decrease, and no rectification will take
place. Now, this is just what we want, for we have
got to avoid rectification and achieve amplification. There
is a potential applied to the grid ; it does not matter how
big or how little it is, it is there and it will produce a

certain corresponding change of anode current. If the circuit is arranged as we have just considered there will be changes for both the positive and negative swings of grid voltage, one an increase and the other a decrease. Now we have put a resistance R in the anode circuit which will impede the flow of anode current. We know by Ohm's law that the total resistance of any circuit varies according to the value of the current flowing in it and the pressure at which it flows.

Voltage Variation

If we were to measure the voltage between the points A and B we should find that it was less than the voltage between the positive pole of the high tension battery and the point B. In other words we have artificially, as it were, made a change of anode to filament voltage. Now, when the grid becomes less negative, there is a greater flow of anode current and consequently the effect of the resistance is greater and the anode filament voltage less. Thus, the more positive the grid becomes the greater the reduction of anode filament voltage in comparison to the voltage which would exist between anode and filament if no resistance were present in the circuit.

Now let us look at this matter in another way. All that we are trying to achieve is a comparative difference of voltage between A—B and +HT—B. So long as we achieve this voltage variation it does not matter in the least whether it is a variation of decrease or increase because we are going to pass it on merely as a variation and not either as an increase or decrease. Very well then, to say that there is a certain difference between the A to B voltage and the +HT to B voltage is surely the same thing as to say that there is a difference between the voltage at one end of the resistance R and at the other. Now, supposing the variation of grid potential is at a value of 1 volt, it may be that each grid swing produced a corresponding fall of anode filament potential of 10 volts, the amplification would be ten times. In other words

there is a voltage variation across the resistance ten times
greater than the grid voltage variation which caused it.
The variation of voltage across the resistance will have
very much the same form as the grid voltage variations
whatever may be the frequency of the latter, and can
consequently be used as an amplified output and connected
to the input circuit of another valve.

We may turn this amplification to account in one of
two different ways, namely, amplification before rectification or amplification after rectification. The former
method is normally referred to as high frequency amplification and the latter low frequency amplification. The

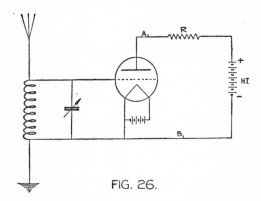

FIG. 26.

reason for these titles should be obvious. We have said
that our object is to increase the signal beyond the point
which can be achieved by the rectifier valve alone. This
does not necessarily mean that the volume of the audible,
that is the rectified, signal is amplified equally by both
methods. In fact, it is here that the two methods differ
diametrically. High frequency amplification has for its
purpose the increase of the feeble oscillations created in
the receiver aerial by those radiated from the aerial of
the distant transmitting station. The function of low
frequency amplification is to amplify the pulses of rectified
anode current, which in our past studies we have considered

only as a motive force for the diaphragm of the telephone receiver. Of course, high frequency amplification does to some extent amplify the signal which becomes audible after it has been passed on to the rectifier valve, because very feeble oscillations from a far distant transmitter may be amplified sufficiently to render them audible, whereas before amplification they could not produce strong enough pulses of rectified anode current to operate the diaphragm of the telephone. Again, feeble oscillations, just strong enough to operate the telephone audibly, may be increased to a point where the audibility of the signal is sufficient to make listening possible without undue concentration. But the point is that one cannot add high frequency amplifying valves one after the other and hope to get ever increasing signals from the telephone because there is a limit to the anode current which the rectifier valve can pass. For the same reason we cannot expect to produce enormous noise in the telephone by applying several stages of high frequency amplification to the already strong oscillations from a near-by transmitting station of great power. To increase the range of the receiver is all that we can expect or that we shall get from high frequency amplification.

High Frequency Amplification

We have seen that a valve can only amplify a certain alternating voltage provided that there is a resistance in the anode circuit. This resistance need not necessarily be in the form of one of the substances which will not readily pass a direct current. It may take the form of a coil offering a high impedance to the flow of an alternating current. We have so far regarded the term impedance merely as an alternative expression of resistance applied to alternating current circuits. To some extent this is quite correct, but a somewhat more detailed examination of the real meaning of impedance is now called for.

We learnt very early in our studies that an inductance coil offered a certain resistance to the passage of a direct current due to the interaction of the lines of force surrounding each separate turn of wire on the coil. Now this resistance increases enormously when we try to pass an alternating current through the coil, because no sooner does the current, travelling in one direction, begin to overcome the resistance offered by the coil, than the direction is reversed and it must needs start all over again flowing in the opposite direction and once more overcome the resistance, and so backwards and forwards perhaps fifty, perhaps a million, times a second according to the frequency of alternation of the supply. This is what we call impedance. The higher the frequency of the supply the higher the impedance of a circuit containing inductance. The greater the current which we pass through an inductance the greater will be its impedance. We know that the maximum current can only flow in a circuit when the

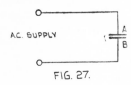

natural frequency of the whole circuit is the same as the frequency of the supply, and that this natural frequency may be controlled by varying the amount of inductance in the circuit. Thus the impedance of a circuit containing inductance

A.C. SUPPLY

FIG. 27.

s determined by the product of the frequency and the inductance of the circuit. Obviously, then, the impedance of a circuit is greatest when the circuit is in resonance with the frequency of the source of supply. A condenser also has impedance to the flow of alternating current. Consider the diagram Fig. 27. A half cycle of alternating E.M.F. will charge up the condenser so that A is positive and B is negative ; the next half cycle will reverse the charge. Now if the condenser is a large one (has a big capacity) and the frequency is fairly high, it is possible that it may not be fully charged before the reversal of direction takes place, and the resistance to the abrupt change of direction is small. If we were to decrease the frequency of the supply so that the condenser had time to become fully charged before the reversal took place, there would be a large difference of potential between the two plates, and the crowd of electrons at A would be loth to leave those at B which were exercising so strong an attractive influence on them. In other words, there would be resistance to the flow of alternating current in the circuit. Suppose that instead of altering the frequency we altered the size (capacity) of the condenser and made it smaller. The same thing will apply because the condenser will charge up more quickly, and the attraction between plates will be present before the change of direction takes place. The impedance of a condenser in an alternating current circuit is dependent upon its capacity and the frequency of the supply, but—just the opposite of the inductance— decreases when either the frequency or the capacity is increased.

From the foregoing discussion it will be obvious that

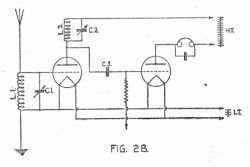

FIG. 28.

any circuit tuned accurately to the frequency of an alternating E.M.F. will offer a high impedance to the flow of current. We have considered the action of a resistance in the anode circuit and the manner in which amplification was achieved with its assistance. Why should we not substitute an accurately tuned inductance for the resistance ? Provided that the frequency of the alternations is sufficiently high to make it an easy matter to construct a coil and condenser which can be tuned simply, such an arrangement may be more effective than a resistance. The important thing to remember is that the impedance of a circuit containing inductance and capacity increases as the natural frequency of the circuit approaches the frequency at which it is desired to pass current through the circuit. Consider the diagram Fig. 28. The aerial circuit is tuned to the frequency of the incoming signal, the valve is not arranged to rectify, and there is another tuned circuit, in series with the anode, offering a high resistance to the passage of current at the particular frequency of the signal. The coil L.2 is in effect the resistance which we had in the anode circuit before, and the voltage variations across it will be of the same form as but of much greater amplitude than the variations of grid voltage which caused them. These amplified voltage variations will be impressed on the grid of the next valve through the condenser C.2. We may put it another way and think of it in terms of electrons. The incoming signal starts a backward and forward movement of electrons in the aerial circuit which controls a much greater movement through the valve, but when the electrons reach the tuned circuit L.2,C.2, they cannot pass easily, so that there is a big crowding of electrons at the anode of the valve, but there is an easy path as far as the grid of the next valve, of which the crowd promptly takes advantage, to have a very much greater effect upon the flow of the electrons from filament to grid of that valve. It is, of course, essential that the capacity of the condenser C.3 should be such as to afford a very low impedance to the frequency of the signal. The form of current is the same and the frequency is unaltered, only the strength has been increased—we have achieved high frequency amplification.

The second valve is arranged in the diagram as a detector ; it may, of course, be another high frequency amplifier. There is a limit to the number of high frequency amplifying valves which can be used, because of the difficulty of preventing self-oscillation owing to stray coupling which may exist between the wires connecting the various pieces of apparatus and because of the feed back which may exist through the inter-electrode capacity of the valves. The circuit may be arranged to provide reaction by coupling a coil inserted in the anode circuit of the detector valve with L.2 in the anode circuit of the amplifier valve. It is sometimes claimed that reaction applied in this way cannot cause re-radiation from the receiver aerial even if the second valve is allowed to oscillate freely. Of course, this is perfectly ridiculous, and although a set of this kind probably radiates less than a single valve detector with reaction coupled directly to the aerial tuning inductance, it is still capable of radiating quite sufficiently to be of considerable annoyance to other listeners in the operator's vicinity. The radiation takes place either through stray coupling in the wiring of the set or through the first valve.

The method of high frequency amplification which we have been discussing is termed " Tuned Anode." It is possible to modify this method by allowing the circuit to be self-tuned—that is to say, by winding the coil L.2 with a large number of turns of very fine wire, the requisite capacity being provided by the total of that which exists between each turn of wire and the next. Provided that the coil is wound so that its natural frequency is exactly the same as that of the signal which it is desired to receive, the circuit will behave in exactly the same manner as a tuned anode circuit, but for a signal of any other frequency the amplification will be less because the impedance will be less. This may be overcome to some extent by taking a number of tappings from the coil, but it involves the use of some form of switch gear so that the desired tapping may be selected without difficulty. Switches and their associated gear are to be avoided in high frequency circuits, and, moreover, an arrangement of this nature produces undesirable effects due to the " dead end " turns of the coil which are not in use. Another method which is sometimes used when a high degree of amplification is not required, and it is desirable to avoid the complication of tuning the anode circuit for each change of station received, is to wind the anode coil with a wire having a higher resistance than the usual copper. This has the added advantage of making the set more stable—that is to say, less prone to burst into oscillation—consequently the low degree of amplification which is obtained by this method may be counteracted to some extent by adding more valves. For the reception of signals of relatively low frequencies of 300,000 cycles and less (1,000 metres and over) the tuned anode method may be replaced by what is termed resistance capacity coupling. It consists simply of replacing the coil L.2 with a high resistance, usually of the cartridge type, and having a D.C. resistance of perhaps 100,000 ohms.

An alternative method of achieving high frequency amplification is that which is shown diagrammatically in Fig. 29. This is generally known as "transformer coupling." The anode coil L1 constitutes the primary of a transformer of which the secondary, L2 is connected across the grid and filament of the next valve. In the

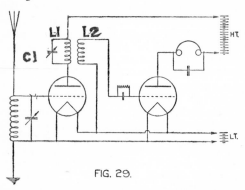

FIG. 29.

diagram the primary is shown as tuned by a condenser C1 to the frequency of the incoming signal, and the amplified voltage variations which are set up across it are faithfully reproduced in the secondary L2 in pursuance of the ordinary laws of coupled circuits and impressed upon the grid of the next valve. The second valve may be arranged as a rectifier or as a second high frequency amplifier. In the diagram it is shown as a cumulative grid rectifier. Reaction may be obtained by connecting the coil in the anode circuit of the rectifier valve and providing variable coupling between it and either the primary or secondary of the transformer. Care must be exercised to connect the

reaction coil the right way round. If it were to be coupled
to the primary, the connection to its two ends would be
the reverse of those required were it to be coupled to the
secondary, because of the change of phase which takes
place in the transformer. The reader will remember that
an induced current always flows in the opposite direction
to that which induced it. In practice, reaction is
seldom necessary in a receiver embodying a well-designed
high frequency amplifier valve, and it may be said that
it is never necessary if more than one high frequency
amplifier valve is used. As has already been pointed out,
there is a tendency to self-oscillation in any high frequency
amplifier which necessitates careful design and adjustment, and the addition of reaction will make it more
difficult to control. In order that the variations of anode
current in L1 may be transferred with the minimum loss
to L2, it is necessary for the two coils to be wound in such
a manner that extremely close coupling is provided between
them. In practice the one is normally wound directly
on top of the other on the same former. Just as was the
case with tuned anode amplification, it is possible to
increase the stability of the amplifier by using a resistance
wire to wind the primary or part of the primary in place
of copper wire, but there will be a loss of amplification.
It is sometimes possible in a transformer-coupled amplifier
to dispense with a tuning condenser if only a very narrow
range of frequencies is required.

The two methods of high frequency amplification which
we have discussed are effective up to a point, but, as we
have already remarked, they have their limitations due
to a lack of stability if more than a certain number of
amplifier valves are used. This lack of stability will
increase as the frequency of the signal which it is desired
to amplify increases. The higher the frequency the greater
will be the tendency of the amplifier to burst into self-
oscillation due to spurious coupling either between connections or through the inter-electrode capacity of the
valve. An extremely ingenious method exists whereby
a very high degree of amplification can be obtained without fear of the loss of stability. It consists fundamentally

of apparatus which reduces the frequency of the incoming
signal to one which is easily amplified and which is sufficiently low to eliminate most of the difficulties normally
attendant upon high frequency amplification. In order to
achieve this object, the heterodyne principle with which
we are already familiar is applied. A local oscillator
generates oscillations at a frequency which differs from
that of the incoming signal and produces a heterodyne or
beat frequency which is low enough to be easily amplified.
It is obvious that it would be impossible to achieve the

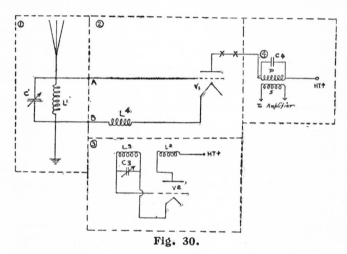

Fig. 30.

desired results if this frequency were made so low as to be
audible, because it would result in the amplification of a
locally created audible note only, and not the incoming
signal. For practical purposes a beat frequency of 75,000
cycles will be found generally satisfactory. The apparatus
used for changing the frequency of an incoming signal is
shown diagrammatically in Fig. 30. It is illustrated as
consisting of four units—(1) a tuner ; (2) a rectifier ; (3) an
oscillator ; and (4) a filter transformer. The aerial circuit
is tuned to the frequency of the desired transmitting station,

which we may take as one million cycles (300 metres), by
the coil L1 and the condenser C1. These oscillations are
impressed on the grid filament circuit of the rectifier. If
we were merely using this as a single valve receiver, unidirectional currents would flow in the anode circuit and a
pair of telephones connecting at XX in unit 2 would render
the signal audible. But we do not want to hear the
signal at this stage ; we want to amplify it first. Therefore we introduce the coil L4 into the grid filament circuit
and couple it to the third unit which is a local oscillator.
If the frequency of this local oscillator is set so that it
generates oscillations at a frequency of either one million
and 75 thousand cycles or 925,000 cycles, the resultant
beat frequency will be 75,000—namely, that which we
require to amplify. Now if we arrange the apparatus so
that L4 is closely coupled to L2, the oscillations in the
local oscillator will appear in the grid circuit and the
receiver will beat with them and produce pulses of anode
current of the required frequency. We have now changed
the frequency to less than one-tenth of its original value.
We cannot claim to make it ten times more easy to amplify,
but we can claim to have removed a very large proportion
of the difficulties attendant upon amplification at so high
a frequency as one million cycles.

The next process is to hand on these reduced frequencies
and pulses to an amplifier, and it is here that we use the
filter transformer. This is a simple straightforward piece
of apparatus usually consisting of an air-cored transformer
wound so that it is tuned to the frequency which we have
selected as the beat or amplification frequency. The
amplifier itself may consist either of transformers with
small iron cores which are quite suitable for amplifying
oscillations of this relatively low frequency, or of some
such arrangement as a resistance capacity amplifier.
The filter transformer is a vital piece of apparatus and
its construction must be very carefully considered. It is
the gateway into the amplifier, and when we come to
consider the application of this type of receiver to the
reception of radio telephony, we shall see how important
it is that the design should be very precise.

Another important point about this method of reception is its extreme selectivity. Why it should be more selective than any other type of receiver is difficult to see at first, but in changing the frequency of one station we are also increasing the separation between it and another station having a frequency nearly the same. Say the wanted station has a frequency of one million cycles and the unwanted station 990,000 cycles. If we reduce the frequency of the wanted station to 75,000 cycles by generating local oscillations of a frequency of one million and 75,000 cycles and apply these local oscillations to the unwanted 990,000 cycles station, we should find that the resultant beat frequency is 1,075,000, minus 990,000, equals 85,000. Thus the difference which at the high frequency was 10,000 cycles is now 85,000 cycles.

It is not necessary at this juncture to illustrate or refer any further to the actual amplifier ; it must follow normal design in every respect. It must, of course, be followed by a second rectifier valve which will rectify the reduced frequency oscillations. The method of high frequency amplification just considered is termed " The Supersonic Heterodyne " method. The name is complicated, but the process is not. It is perhaps the most simple form of amplification which it is possible to devise. It requires only two tuning adjustments—namely, the setting of the condenser C1 to tune to the incoming oscillations, and the setting of the condenser C2 to tune the locally generated oscillations. After this, the receiver, so to speak, does everything by itself. One very important point is that this type of receiver should never in any circumstances be used on an outside aerial. It must always be attached to a small frame aerial. As we have seen, it relies for its proper action on the generation of oscillation, and if it is attached to an outside aerial these will inevitably be radiated and will cause interference with other receivers in the vicinity. The radiation from a small frame aerial is so small that there is little possibility of causing any interference with other people.

STABILISING THE H.F. AMPLIFIER

While the supersonic heterodyne method is effective
in overcoming some of the difficulties attendant upon high
frequency amplification, the apparatus required is somewhat expensive. If considered absolutely literally it
really cannot claim to be a high frequency amplifier since
the whole principle of its operation is based upon the
reduction of the frequency to a relatively low one before
amplification takes place, and therefore reducing the
effect of stray capacities which are harmful at higher
frequencies.

Let us suppose now that we wish to obtain the maximum
possible amplification without changing the frequency.
The problems which we are up
against are three. First, there are
what we may term the "shunt stray
capacities" which exist in a high
frequency circuit. Consider the
diagram, Fig. 31. A resistance R
is in the anode circuit. Now we
know that the essential condition
of amplification is that there should
be a high impedance of the plate
circuit outside the valve. At a

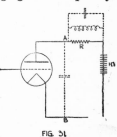

FIG. 31

very high frequency of the order of a million cycles,
relatively very little amplification would be obtained
by the arrangement in the diagram because stray
capacities represented by the dotted line and condenser
between A and B would afford a very low impedance at
this frequency. If we replace the resistance R by a
certain value of inductance we know that we can
obtain a very high amplification at the one particular
frequency at which the inductance affords the maximum
impedance in conjunction with its self capacity and the
stray shunt capacity between A B. Similarly, if we tune
this inductance with a parallel condenser as shown in
dotted line on the diagram a very high degree or
amplification may be obtained over the certain band of

frequencies to which the circuit may be tuned by this combination of inductance and capacity. Included in the total capacity is, of course, the stray shunt capacity between A and B. We may say then that the first difficulty is overcome by tuning the anode circuit.

The second problem is, however, very much more difficult to overcome. In every valve there must be a capacity between the grid and plate of the valve—in other words, there must be inter-electrode capacity. We have already discussed in general terms the danger of inter-electrode capacity in affording a path for unwanted reaction effects resulting in self-oscillation of the amplifier, but it has another adverse effect in that it affords a bypass to earth for the high frequency oscillations which are trying to pass on to the next amplifying valve or detector as the case may be. This inter-electrode capacity has been the bugbear of radio engineers for the past ten years, and many and various efforts have been made to devise means of counteracting its effect. The physical construction of the valve has a great deal to do with its inter-electrode capacity, and much has been done to reduce the effect by dispensing with the ordinary 4-pin arrangement in which all the electrodes are brought through a narrow sealed pinch at the bottom of the evacuated tube and constructing the valve to resemble a test tube bringing the connections from the electrodes to metal lugs at the two ends and two sides of the tube. This has the advantage not only of reducing the capacity between the leads from the electrodes inside the valve itself, but also of enabling the design of the set to allow of a much wider space between the external leads to and from the valve than is possible with the ordinary 4-pin socket arrangement. Even though the capacity between leads has been materially reduced by this method, there is still the considerable capacity between the actual electrodes of the valves themselves.

The method which has been generally used up to a very recent date consists of an arrangement to counteract this capacity effect by connecting a small condenser between the plate and the grid of the valve. Original research work in this direction was carried out by Professor

Heseltine, a distinguished American scientist and research worker, who gave the name to his arrangement of the "Neutrodyne" receiver. Since his earlier experiments many different arrangements have been tried, but most have been found to be too complicated and the arrangement used to-day varies very little from his original design.

The circuit in Fig. 32 shows the first arrangement which was tried to effect neutralisation of inter-electrode capacity of the valve. The arrangement consists of a tuned anode

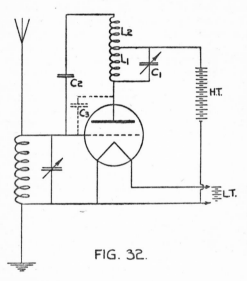

FIG. 32.

high frequency amplifier. Coil L1 is the anode coil tuned by the variable condenser C1. Coil L2 is connected in series with the anode coil and joined through the condenser C2 to the grid of the valve. Coupling between the two coils is variable and when this is adjusted properly the current fed back through the condenser C2 can be made equal to the current passing through the dotted line condenser C3 which represents the inner-electrode capacity of the valve. If the current in these two condensers is equal it is obvious that there can be no voltage variations on the grid due to stray capacity coupling.

A later development of this arrangement is shown in Fig. 33 where the coupling is of the transformer type. The primary and neutralising winding are wound as one coil on a former with a tapping point for the positive H.T., the secondary of the transformer being wound immediately over the primary. This is a normal form of connection of a neutrodyne circuit as incorporated in a modern receiver.

The third problem with which we have to contend is the effect of spurious coupling between the connecting wires running to and from the valve and other apparatus in the receiver. There is only one way of preventing these

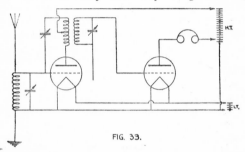

FIG. 33.

effects and that is the exercise of extreme care in the design of the receiver. Wires should be kept as short as possible and not allowed to run parallel to one another.

Before leaving our discussions on high frequency amplification there is one matter which must be touched upon.

A revolutionary discovery has removed for all time the need for compromise in the design and construction of high frequency amplifiers. This discovery has become known as the " screened " valve. Many readers will no doubt have taken the opportunity to examine one of the new screened valves for themselves. The object of the valve is to combine a maximum degree of amplification per stage with the elimination of any tendency to self-oscillation of the amplifier due to inter-electrode capacity.

We learnt in our studies of high frequency amplification that the valves of a high frequency amplifier could not normally be operated in the most advantageous manner without incurring risk of self-oscillation. We studied various means by which this risk could be reduced, but all of them constituted some form of compromise which resulted in minimising the degree of amplification which could be obtained.

Disregarding the supersonic method which really falls into a field quite apart, the most satisfactory method is undoubtedly the neutrodyne method, but even this is by no means certain, and it has an important disadvantage. When a circuit is neutralised by this method, that is to say the inter-electrode capacity of the valves is matched by the neutralising condenser, a considerable amount of time and care has to be expended on the process. Now, however carefully valves are constructed so that each one of a certain type matches the others, it is impossible, even with the most up-to-date methods of manufacture, to ensure exactly equal spacing of the electrodes, consequently the inter-electrode capacity of every valve varies. Therefore, if the filament of a valve breaks, or if for any other reason it is desired to change the valve for a new one, the whole process of balancing the circuit with a neutralising condenser has to be repeated. The neutralising condenser is also responsible for balancing the stray anode to filament shunt capacity. Obviously this capacity alters if the coupling, whether it be a transformer or a tuned inductance, is altered. For instance, the shunt capacity with a coil in the anode circuit, suitable for tuning to the normal broadcast band of 300-600 metres, will be different from that when a coil is inserted to cover the wavelength of Daventry 5XX. If the coupling is altered to accommodate wavelength changes, it is again necessary to rebalance the whole circuit. The new screened valve dispenses with the necessity for such exterior aids to stability. Its construction is similar to that of the ordinary three-electrode valve, with the exception that a fourth electrode is introduced in the form of an outer grid between the normal grid and anode.

The outer grid may consist either of a fine mesh weave of wire or of a perforated metal plate. Its diameter is nearly equal to the inside diameter of the glass tube, and attached to its outside edge is a metal ring arranged to lie closely against the inside circumference of the glass tube. The anode of the valve differs from that which is normally found in the three-electrode valve, in that it consists of a flat plate and is not cylindrical. In the original design the connections to the valve are taken out at its two ends, the two terminals of the filament and the one of the inner grid protrude from one end of the tube and the terminals of the plate and outer grid from the other end. In some later designs this arrangement has been modified.

The introduction of this outer grid provides a screen between the normal grid and anode of the valve, thus preventing to a large degree the possibility of feed-back due to inter-electrode capacity.

Obviously this screening effect cannot be absolute. If it were, the screen would have to be of solid metal, and there could be no passage of electrons from grid to anode, but it is so effectual as to reduce the anode to grid capacity to an almost negligible amount, provided that ordinary care is taken in the design of the amplifier as a whole, so that interaction between the tuned circuits and connecting wires is avoided.

For this purpose it is best to screen each stage of amplification in a copper box. The valve may be arranged so that one end protrudes at each side of this copper screen, and in such a way that the outer ring of the screened grid is close to and concentric with a hole cut in the copper screen.

Almost as important a property of the screened valve as this elimination of feed-back through inter-electrode capacity is the relatively large amplification which can be achieved with this type of valve. In a sense the one is consequent upon the other. The difficulty with the three-electrode valve was that the maximum magnification obtainable could not be used because the greater the magnification the greater the feed-back, consequently the greater the tendency to self-oscillation. But in addition to overcoming this difficulty, the screened valve actually gives higher magnification than the three-electrode valve because its internal resistance is higher.

Because the screen grid is not solid there will still be some feed back. If, however, a suitable arrangement of tuned circuits is used, this feed back can be kept below a point where oscillations will be set up in the amplifier itself, and therefore provides a reaction effect increasing the total amplification of the amplifier. Here then are two good reasons why greater amplification can be obtained with the screened valve than with the normal three-electrode valve. But there is another and even more important reason. To induce feed back effects we put a screen between the inner or control grid and the anode. To be effective this screen must be connected to some potential point in the circuit. Normally, the screen grid is connected to a point on the high tension battery, in other words it is given a positive potential.

Now it is obvious that this must have considerable effect on the characteristic of the valve. To understand this we must revert for a moment to our studies of the characteristics of three-electrode valves, page 67. The voltage amplification factor of a valve is represented by the ratio of change of grid volts to change of anode volts for a given change of anode current, but there is another important characteristic called the " mutual conductance " which is an expression of the change of anode current for a given change of grid potential.

Now in order that the greatest amplification can be obtained from any one valve, both the voltage amplification factor and the mutual conductance must be as high as possible. The closer the mesh of the grid the greater will be the amplification factor, because a smaller grid voltage variation will achieve the same results in change of anode current. It is obvious, therefore, that the higher the resistance of the valve the higher the amplification factor, since the filament to anode resistance depends upon the mesh of the grid.

Examine the curves, Fig. 37. These represent anode

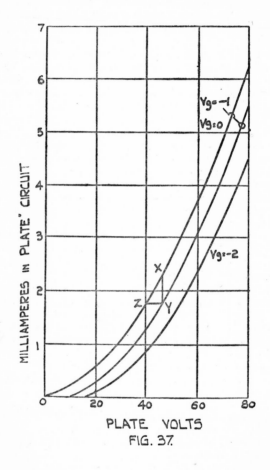

FIG. 37.

volt-anode current characteristics of a standard type of three-electrode valve taken at three different grid potentials. It will be observed that at one point two of the curves are joined by the lines XY and YZ forming a triangle.

The line ZY, read along the lower horizontal line of plate volts represents the voltage amplification of the

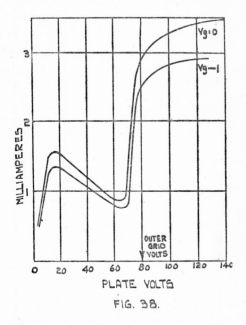

FIG. 38.

valve, because if the plate voltage is changed by an amount equivalent to the distance between Z and Y, the same anode current is registered by reducing the grid volts from zero to minus one.

The line from X to Y obviously represents the mutual conductance because it shows directly the increase in anode current resulting from increase in grid volts from minus one to zero. The resistance of the valve is of course ZY divided by XY.

Now turn to Fig. 38 which illustrates the anode volts anode current characteristics of a four-electrode screened valve at two different grid potentials. The screen grid is fixed at a potential of plus 80 volts. It will be seen that when positive potential is applied to the anode a flow of current commences and the curve rises up to a point where the anode volts are about +20. Thereafter it falls steeply. This is due to the action of the screen grid which has previously allowed a certain number of electrons to trickle through the anode. At the point where the curve starts to go downwards, the screen grid being at a higher potential than the anode, secondary electrons are produced owing to bombardment of the anode, and are attracted back to the screen grid, causing a rise of current in its circuit and a subtraction of current from the anode circuit. From the point where the anode volts are nearly equal to the screen volts the curve starts to straighten out, thereafter rising rapidly to a point where the anode volts exceed the grid volts. After this point the curve straightens out to a long steady rise, which means that it is tending to saturate, but only gradually.

Now apply the same triangle to this part of the curve, above +100 plate volts, as we applied to the curve of the three-electrode valve, and we find that a very different state of affairs exist. The amplification factor is several times greater, and the mutual conductance is at least as great, consequently of course the resistance is very much higher. It is best to operate the four-electrode screened valve with about 120 volts on the plate and 80 volts on the inner grid. With this arrangement and zero grid volts, the internal resistance of the valve is approximately 175,000 ohms, the amplification factor is 112 and the mutual conductance is .64 milliamps per volt.

Here then we have a valve which is capable of tremendous magnification, without excessive H.T. volts, combined with stability. We have only dealt very summarily with an extraordinarily interesting subject, and it would be beyond the scope of this book to go more deeply into the matter. For those who wish to follow it up themselves, the writer would recommend them to read a recently published volume entitled " The Shielded Four-Electrode Valve," by Captain H. J. Round, M.C., M.I.E.E

CHAPTER VI

THE VALVE AS A LOW FREQUENCY AMPLIFIER

*Alternative methods of Low Frequency Amplification—
Transformer design and construction.*

WE will now turn our attention to the subject
of low frequency amplification—that is to
say, amplification of a received signal after
the process of rectification.

Our object is to amplify those average pulses of unidirectional current which we considered in our earlier
studies as flowing in the anode circuit of a rectifier valve
and actuating the diaphragm of a telephone receiver at
an audible frequency. Now the problem of low frequency
amplification differs in many particulars from that of
high frequency, though fundamentally it is governed
by the general principles which apply to valve amplification.
A high impedance in the anode circuit in relation to the
impedance of the valve itself is, of course, still neccessary
for effective amplification, but we are not now primarily
concerned with the problem of obtaining the highest
degree of amplification at one particular frequency ; in
fact the very reverse is the case, since it is now our object
to amplify all audible frequencies. Whether we are
listening to the speech and music of a broadcasting station
or receiving morse signals either consisting of the damped
or continuous waves, the low frequency amplifier must,
if it is to be efficient, amplify all the frequencies concerned
equally.

For example, supposing we were to listen to one spark
station, having a frequency of a thousand cycles, which

was distant and was only just audible after, say, two stages of low frequency amplification, we might find that an inefficient low frequency amplifier which failed to give equal amplification at all low frequencies would lose the audible signal from that station altogether if the operator at the transmitter altered the frequency of his spark to 300 cycles. Similarly, for the reception of continuous waves the low frequency amplifier must cover a large range of audible frequencies in order that we may select any required heterodyne note. A low frequency amplifier, then, must give proper and equal amplification to all these frequencies or the sounds reproduced in the telephone or loud speaker will differ from those at the point of origin and become distorted. This process of amplifying all frequencies equally is called the frequency characteristic of the amplifier. A perfect frequency characteristic plotted as a graph having frequencies as one co-ordinate and voltage amplification as the other would be represented theoretically by a straight line. In practice it is seldom possible to get an absolutely straight line frequency characteristic, but we can get very close to it.

Read in conjunction with our recent consideration of high frequency amplification, it may seem to the reader rather like accomplishing the impossible, but there is another important difference between low and high frequency amplification which makes the achievement of even amplification at all audible frequencies much less difficult than it appears at first sight. Reverting for a moment to our study of high frequency amplification, it will be remembered that one of the greatest difficulties which we had to overcome was the stray shunt capacity of the anode circuit and the capacity path provided between the electrodes of the valve, both of which tended to reduce the total voltage amplification by providing an easy path for the oscillations which would otherwise have been available to be impressed in the form of voltage variations of the grid of the next valve.

In the case of low frequency amplification, neither of these difficulties have to be overcome because the capacity either from anode to earth or through the valve is so small as to offer an extremely high impedance to oscillations having frequencies within the audible range and is therefore a help rather than a hindrance. Another but less important point is that there is less likelihood of low frequency oscillation between stages of a low frequency amplifier consequently allowing a greater number of stages to be used with safety.

Up to three stages of low frequency amplification can be handled without difficulty ; after this, however, special measures have to be taken, but we need not discuss these, as it is seldom found in practice that more than three stages of amplification are required ; in fact, a well designed two stage amplifier will usually give all the signal strength required. Uneven amplification is not the only cause of distortion in low frequency amplifiers. Another is overloaded valves and associated coupling apparatus. The only prevention for this is the use of the right type of valve, having a straight anode current characteristic. Another and very usual form of distortion is produced if grid current is allowed to flow, that is to say, if the positive impulses on the grid become of so high a potential as to allow current to flow round the circuit. This can be prevented by the application of an artificial negative grid potential or " grid bias " as it is generally called. This must be done circumspectly or we shall produce a state of affairs where the valve rectifies instead of amplifying. The correct grid potential for different types of valves is generally indicated by the manufacturers and should be carefully observed. Of course, the biasing potential will vary considerably with the position of the valve in the amplifier. More negative must be applied to the grid of the last amplifier valve than to the first because the voltage variations are greater.

The above are, in general terms, the conditions prerequisite to faithful and undistorted amplification of electrical impulses passing in a receiving circuit at frequencies within the audible limit. We must consider these impulses as wave motion just as we did the high-frequency oscillations before rectification. We must take it for granted that the rectifier whether it be a valve or a crystal gives us a wave of equal strength if the frequency is 30 per second or 300, and the problem with which we are now concerned is to maintain that equality of strength throughout the process of amplification.

From our earlier discussions we know that practically any valve will amplify if connected in a suitable manner with certain other apparatus, but that is not to say that it will do so correctly or faithfully. Suppose that we select a valve having a close mesh grid and ask it to amplify a note having a frequency of 256 cycles per second—this note happens to be the middle C of a piano. We must, of

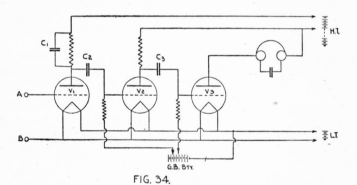

FIG. 34.

course, arrange something to supply the necessary impedance in the anode circuit. The first half cycle we will say is positive. The grid becomes positive and anode current flows, but if the positive voltage on the grid is large grid current will flow (all the more so if, as in the case we have selected, a valve with a close mesh grid), with the result that the anode current is less than it should be. Half a cycle later the grid receives a negative voltage. The valve has a close mesh grid, so the barrier is a very effective one, and there is a very large fall in anode current out of all proportion to the increase which resulted from the positive half cycle. The form of the wave is distorted. We apply an artificial auxiliary

negative grid potential to stop grid current flowing, and
what happens ? It is true that we have insured that no
grid current will flow during the positive half circles, but
we have made the negative half cycles set up an even more
effective barrier for the electrons to try to struggle through.
In point of fact we shall probably find that we have
produced a state of affairs where there is only anode
current flowing during the positive half cycles and none
at all during the negative half cycles, thus instead of
variations of anode current we have produced a state of
affairs where the current stops and starts with each positive
half cycle ; in other words, the valve is rectifying instead
of amplifying. Obviously, this valve is no good at all for
the job, so we must try another which has an open mesh
grid and a characteristic curve with a long straight portion.
This, then, is the first step towards distortionless amplification. Choose the right type of valve.

There are three methods of coupling between valves
which may be used in low-frequency amplification.
The first and undoubtedly the best is very similar to
one which we have already considered in connection with
high frequency amplification. The method is generally
referred to as " Resistance capacity " amplification. Fig.
34 shows a two-stage resistance capacity amplifier in diagrammatic form. Properly adjusted an amplifier of this
type will give absolutely undistorted amplification of all
frequencies. This is because the resistances R1 and
R2 will offer a practically uniform impedance to all
frequencies which it may be desired to pass through the
amplifier. This type of amplifier has, however, two
serious disadvantages in comparison with the other types
which we will consider later. The first is that the amplification which can be obtained from each stage is relatively
low. This is because the ohmic resistance of the resistances
which we use must be kept low enough to allow of sufficient
anode voltage for the valve, and cannot therefore be as
high as we should like to make them in order to offer
a higher impedance in the anode circuit. While the
impedance is to all intents and purposes equal at all
low frequencies it is not as high as that which can be

obtained from other methods. The other disadvantage is that a very much larger plate voltage (H.T. Battery) must be used in order to overcome the ohmic resistance of the anode resistance and still operate the valve at the plate voltage for which it was designed. Now let us examine the circuit and the manner of its operation. R1 and 2 are the anode resistances. C2 and 3 are the coupling condensers ; in a resistance low frequency amplifier the capacity of these condensers must be such as will afford a low impedance to sound frequencies, normally a value of from .05 to .2 microfarad will be found to be satisfactory.

The condenser C1 is what is termed a bye-pass condenser. It is not concerned in any way with the amplification of sound frequencies, but is there to provide a path for the high frequency component of the anode current variations. In our study of the rectification of high frequency oscillation we learnt that the audible signal consisted of an average increase or decrease of unidirectional high frequency pulses, according to the method of rectification used. The purpose of the condenser C1 is therefore to afford an easier path for the high frequency pulses than that is provided by the resistance R1 and condenser C2 The condenser is accordingly of small capacity, offering very little impedance to the high frequency pulses and a very high impedance to those of audible frequency. C1 will have a capacity of about .0001. The action of the amplifier itself is simple to follow. The low-frequency voltage variations across the resistance R1 are impressed upon the grid of V2 through C2 setting up amplified voltage variations across R2, which are again passed on to the grid of V3 and heard in the telephone or loud speaker connected in the anode circuit of the latter.

The reader should now have in his mind certain important facts. Firstly, that a resistance capacity amplifier is practically distortionless because the impedance of a resistance to alternating current is to all intents aperiodic ; that is to say, it does not vary with the frequency of the voltage variations with whose amplification it is concerned.

Secondly, that the impedance of a condenser or an inductance is definitely periodic and does vary with the frequency
of alternation.   Thirdly, that a resistance amplifier does
not give a very high voltage amplification per stage because, although the impedance of the anode resistance is
aperiodic it is not high.   Fourthly, that with this type of
amplifier increased anode voltage must be applied to the
valve in order to overcome the ohmic resistance of the
anode resistances.

Now supposing we substitute for the resistance an
inductance.   We know that reactance of an inductance
to an alternating current varies with the frequency of that
current and that the lower the frequency the higher must
be the inductance to obtain a given impedance.   To
amplify low frequency voltage variations such as correspond
to sounds of audible frequency an inductance coil of
enormous proportions would be necessary ; the coil would
in fact be so large as to become quite unwieldy and incapable of being accommodated in the normal space
available for receiving apparatus.   We therefore resort to a
compromise and wind a coil on an iron core.   We know
that a current passing through a conductor produces
lines of force round that conductor.   If the current is an
alternating one, and the conductor is a coil of wire, there
is a constant state of decreasing and increasing interacting
lines of force about the turns of the coil and about the coil
as a whole.   This varying density of magnetic field is
generally referred to as magnetic flux.   In the case of an
ordinary coil without a core the flux must travel in air,
the provision of a core localises a large proportion of the
flux in the immediate vicinity of the turns of wire composing
the coil, and therefore increases its density in that area.
The effect of this is twofold, firstly, it increases the total
inductance of the coil, and, secondly, it makes the whole
inductance slightly aperiodic, considerably more so than
the coil would be without the core.   Such an arrangement
of a single coil wound round an iron core is usually termed
a " choke " coil and may be substituted for the anode
resistance of the resistance capacity amplifier, with the
result that greater amplification per stage is obtained

because of the higher reactance which will be afforded by the chokes.

If the chokes are very carefully designed it is possible to obtain nearly as distortionless amplification as can be achieved by the resistance method. The usual process is to wind a coil on the centre of a core such as is illustrated in the diagram, Fig. 35. There will, of course, be certain losses in the iron core itself. These losses are due to a variety of somewhat complicated causes and are outside

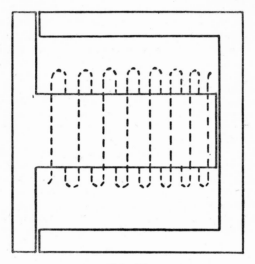

Fig. 35.

the scope of this elementary book, consequently we need not concern ourselves with them at the moment. They may be reduced by constructing the core of a number of thin laminations instead of from a solid piece of metal. Another disadvantage of this method in a comparison to the resistance arrangement is that a certain amount of distortion may be introduced as a result of eddy currents which are set up in the core. The elimination of this distortion is entirely a question of very careful design of the choke coil and core. On the other hand, one of the difficulties inherent to resistance capacity amplification disappears entirely with the choke capacity method—that is, the plate voltage has not to be increased as it had in the case of the resistance amplifier to overcome the ohmic resistance of the anode resistances. This is because the direct current resistance of the choke consists only of the resistance of the wire composing the coil, which is negligible.

A choke amplifier may introduce distortion due to the resonant frequency of the choke itself. We learnt in our earlier studies that any circuit containing inductance and capacity had a resonant frequency which was dependent on the values of those components. The choke coil is an inductance and it contains self capacity due to the proximity of the turns of wire composing it. The total of this inductance and capacity may be such as to produce a resonant frequency at which the choke will offer a higher impedance than to other frequencies which it is desired to amplify. If the choke is designed so that it has a high impedance to all the frequencies which it is desired to amplify in relation to the resistance of the valve, the extra impedance which is afforded at the resonant frequency will not introduce very serious distortion, but if the choke is badly designed, or is of an unsuitable type for the valves being used, then considerable distortion may result. The remedy is, of course, to change the choke for a more suitable one, but if this cannot be done it is possible to reduce the distortion by connecting a resistance in parallel with the choke coil. This will make the choke more aperiodic, but it will also reduce the effective amplification because the total impedance to any frequency of the choke and resistance in parallel will not be as high as that of the choke alone. The operation of the amplifier is in all respects similar to the resistance amplifier and the arrangement of the circuit is the same, except that the anode resistance shown in Fig. 34, page 125, are replaced by chokes.

And now we come to the third method of low frequency

amplification. We have discussed the choke-coupled amplifier and found that a higher degree of amplification could be obtained with it than with the resistance method, but that it was more liable to introduce distortion. Now supposing we took a choke coil wound on an iron core, and instead of passing on the amplified voltage variations through a condenser to the grid of the next valve, we wound another coil on top of the choke and connected one end of it to the grid of the next valve and the other to the filament, we should have something of the same piece of apparatus as we used in a transformer-coupled high frequency amplifier,

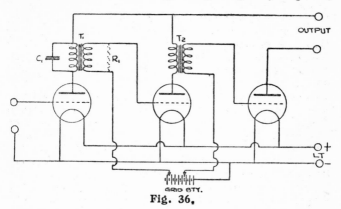

Fig. 36.

except that now the transformer has an iron core which is common to both primary and secondary winding. A transformer coupled amplifier has one great advantage over the other two kinds—namely that much higher amplification may be obtained per stage. On the other hand, it has all the disadvantages of the choke but in greater degree, since both primary and secondary are open to all the difficulties of design and tendencies to distortion, and in addition there are some difficulties to be overcome which are peculiar to the transformer alone.

The usual method of constructing transformers is to wind the primary and the secondary each in several

sections. The same type of core as was illustrated in Fig.
35 is in general use for transformers. The sections
of the primary and secondary are placed on the core
alternately, first a primary section then a secondary
section, and so on. It is of the utmost importance that
each primary section should be insulated from each
secondary. A thin layer of waxed paper is often used.
After assembly the primary sections are connected together
in series and the secondary sections likewise. The transformer amplifier can give higher amplification per stage
because the voltage variations across the primary will
produce greater voltage variations in the secondary if
the latter is wound with a greater number of turns of wire.
Say that the secondary coil has four times more turns
than the primary, we should obtain voltage variations
four times as great. Thus if the primary gives an amplification of a value ten, the total amplification impressed
on the grid of the next valve would have a value 40. This
assumes no losses in the transformer, a condition which is
unfortunately seldom achieved even with the most careful
design. We must remember that the losses in the core
are now twofold, effecting both primary and secondary,
and that there are now two inductances both having self
capacity and consequently in both there is a resonant
frequency at which a greater reactance is afforded to the
voltage variations than at any other frequency. The
two resonant frequencies are different because the inductance of both coils is different unless the transformer
is wound with a 1 to 1 turns ratio which in practice is
seldom the case. The core, although of similar type to
that which we considered in connection with the choke
coil requires to be of specially careful design. Fig. 36
shows a typical transformer coupled amplifier. It is not
normally practicable to use more than two stages of
amplification. T1 and T2 are the coupling transformers.
It is, of course, still necessary to apply a negative bias to
the grids of the valves in order that they may be operated
on the most effective part of their characteristic curves.
Cl is a by pass condenser. If there is difficulty in avoiding
distortion due to the resonant frequency of the primary

or secondary of the transformer this may be overcome by shunting the secondary with the resistance R1, although some reduction in the strength of signal will result.

Although we are dealing with low frequencies we must not neglect to take some precaution against spurious coupling between the components of the amplifier which may give rise to low frequency oscillation. It is not necessary to space the wiring and the components with such care as in a high frequency amplifier, but some precautions are essential ; for instance, it is bad practice to place two transformers very close together with the turns of wire composing the coils parallel to one another. Do not forget to pick the right type of valve and to arrange the circuit so that it is operated on the proper part of its characteristic curve. A valve in the last stage of an amplifier will require more negative grid bias than the others because it will have greater voltage variations to deal with. If a loud speaker is to be operated the last valve will have to provide quite considerable power quite apart from the process of amplification. We must pick a valve with a long straight portion to the left of the zero grid volts line and ensure that the maximum negative potential which the grid receives from the incoming alternations does not, when added to the auxiliary negative potential, produce a value which will work the valve on the flat or horizontal part of the bottom bend allowing rectification to take place. We must also ensure that the maximum positive swing of the grid does not allow grid current to flow. We must therefore use a low impedance valve having a very open mesh grid which will give a large output of power. To ensure the latter we must apply a high potential to the anode.

CHAPTER VII

THE TRANSMISSION OF WIRELESS TELEPHONY

The Microphone—Studios—Microphone Amplifiers—Modulation

WE have covered a great deal of the ground involved in a study of the problems concerned with the transmission and reception of wireless signals generally. A great deal of the ground, but by no means all. Still, we should by now have acquired a working knowledge of most of the important problems. The object of this book is only to cover the ground quite superficially. Let us now apply the knowledge we have acquired to the processes involved in broadcasting the speech and music which go to make up the programmes we have become accustomed to accept as a part of our daily life.

We know from our early studies that the radiation of electro-magnetic waves can only be achieved if they are propagated at a very high frequency, much too high to be audible. Therefore, taking for granted that we can change the sound waves produced by the speaker or player at the broadcasting station into corresponding electrical waves, it would not be possible to radiate them directly as such. Consequently, there are two very distinct and separate processes involved. Firstly, the propagation of continuous waves of a high enough frequency to be radiated, and secondly the conversion of sound waves into some form of electrical impulse, which can be superimposed upon the high frequency waves and " carried " by them to the distant receiver.   It is because of this that the high frequency radiation of a telephony transmitter is sometimes referred to as its " carrier wave."   In super-imposing the low or sound frequencies on the carrier wave the latter is said to be " modulated."   The whole apparatus, therefore, must be such that the carrier wave can be modulated at all frequencies within the audible limit—say 50 to 10,000 cycles, and that the smallest sound wave is capable of producing the required modulation.   The instrument used to convert sound waves into this electrical equivalent is termed a " microphone."

THE MICROPHONE

In the early days of broadcasting a type of microphone was used closely resembling the ordinary land-line telephone instrument which one uses in one's office and house daily.   It was not, however, designed for handling a very wide range of frequencies, because it did not need to do so.   The range of frequencies covered by the human voice in speech is relatively small, and lies about the middle of the audible range.   When it came to dealing with all the frequencies covered by—shall we say ?—a symphony orchestra, the instrument was soon found wanting, because both the high and the low frequencies outside the range it was accustomed and designed to handle were not reproduced as faithfully or with as much strength as the middle range.   The principle on which it operated, however, was in some respects the right one, and it is an interesting fact that after many alternatives have been tried the type in current use at many broadcasting stations is a reversion to the same principle, albeit somewhat modified in construction.   The principle of operation relies on the fact that the resistance to the flow of an electrical current, through granules of carbon varies in direct relation to the density with which the granules are packed.   For instance, take a quantity of loose carbon granules and place them in a container made of some insulating material, having a metal bottom on which the

granules may rest. Now place a thin and very light
metal plate exactly fitting the inside diameter of the
container on the top of the granules, connect a wire to
each end of the appliance that is, one to the fixed metal
bottom of the container and the other to the loose plate
resting on the granule. Now connect the other two ends
of the wires, through an ampère meter, to the two poles
of a battery, and it will be found that the current flowing
in the circuit will vary as different degrees of pressure are
applied to the granules by pressing the top loose plate
downwards so that the density is increased or decreased.
If then we enclose some loose carbon granules behind a
sensitive diaphragm and arrange the instrument in such
a way that the diaphragm will vibrate in response to
impinging air waves caused by sound, we have a piece of
apparatus which will convert sounds into alternating
electrical currents. If a note on the piano is struck—say
middle " C "—256 air displacements per second strike
the diaphragm of the microphone, the density of the
granules is varied 256 times per second, and the current
flowing in the circuit to which the microphone is attached
varies in sympathy. The extent to which the current
will vary each side of a given constant will depend upon
the strength with which the air waves strike the diaphragm.
Thus, if the note on the piano is struck with the loud pedal
depressed the current variations in the microphone circuit
will be large, but if the soft pedal is depressed the variation
will be small. Thus the microphone records (in the form
of current variation in its associated circuit) not only
the original sound but the strength of the sound at the
point of origin as well. Various other types of microphone have been and are being tried. One type which
is obsolescent, but still in use at quite a number of broadcasting stations, operates on an entirely different principle.
A very light coil wound with extremely fine wire is suspended in the field of a strong electro magnet. The
impinging sound waves actually move the coil (which
is so light as practically to constitute a diaphragm) and
its position is varied in the field of the magnet, with
consequent variation of the current in any circuit to

which it is connected. Another type of which we may expect to hear much in the future is the condenser microphone. There is one fixed metal plate, in front of which is suspended a very thin plate acting as a diaphragm. As the diaphragm moves so the two plates are momentarily nearer together and further apart, varying the total capacity of the circuit.

STUDIOS

The studio itself must, of course, be specially constructed in order to eliminate undesirable echo effects and other forms of distortion inherent to confined spaces. The ideal place to produce an absolutely pure and undistorted sound wave is in an open space where there is no other sound and no solid substance to reflect or distort the wave. This is obviously impracticable. The next best thing is to adapt the necessarily confined space in which the sound has to be originated. For this purpose the walls and the ceilings of studios are usually draped with some loose material which is so constructed as to be adjustable, so that the degree of damping can be varied. Of course, the problem is a far more complicated one than can be dealt with by having just one studio which can be adapted to each type of performance. The requisite acoustics of a studio used for talks are so different from those of a studio used for large orchestral performances that no amount of adjustment of drapery would produce good results for both types of performance ; consequently, the more studios with which a broadcasting station is equipped the better, each being adapted for some particular kind of work.

Latterly, it has been realised that the elimination of the echo effect in the studio leaves something wanting in the resultant reproduction. The human ear is accustomed to a certain amount of echo ; and the elimination of it, although it would not actually introduce distortion of the sound wave, would produce a sound which was not absolutely normal. Means exist at many broadcasting

stations whereby echo can be introduced to the transmission where none exists in the studio in which the performance is taking place. This is done by passing the
electrical impulses, generated by the microphone in response
to the sound waves, through an amplifier and loud speaker
situated in a room apart from the studio which is without
any damping, and has a large degree of echo. A second
microphone is suspended in front of the loud speaker to
pick up the echoey reproduction from the latter. At
the appropriate stage in the process of transmission, the
output of this microphone is superimposed on the output of
the original studio microphone.

An extremely important matter connected with the
faithful transmission of the sounds radiated in the studio
is the proper balancing of the performers, where the item
of the programme is a concerted one. The situation in
the studio of the players composing an orchestra is a critical
matter. For example, the players constituting the brass
section of an orchestra must take up a certain position in
relation to the microphone, the wood wind section a
different position, and so on. This balancing of an orchestra
in a studio has become a science which has grown up
with the science of broadcasting. It would be beyond
the scope of this book to go more deeply into questions
of studio construction and technique, but it is as well
for the reader to have the foregoing outline of the
processes involved in the faithful conversion of sounds into
electrical impulses. For those who wish to study these
aspects of the transmission of radio telephony, some
excellent articles have been written by the leading experts
in studio acoustics and technique and will be found in the
B.B.C. Handbook, 1928.

Now the microphone itself, although an extremely
sensitive piece of apparatus, and one according an amazing
degree of equality in the treatment of all of the several
amplitudes and frequencies of sound waves with which
it must deal, does not reproduce them in the form of large
electrical impulses. They are infinitesimally small in
comparison with the impulses which are produced by the
ordinary commercial microphone used for land line tele-

phone work ; consequently, the impulses must be amplified before they can be utilised to modulate the high frequency continuous waves generated by the transmitter.

MICROPHONE AMPLIFIERS

The degree of amplification depends upon the power required to accomplish this modulation effectively. The greater the radiating power of the transmitter the greater will be the amplification required.

The greater part of this amplification is a function of the transmitting apparatus itself, part of which consists of a low frequency amplifier. The minute electrical impulses generated by the microphone must, however, be amplified to some degree before they reach the input of the amplifier at the transmitter. Furthermore, some means of control must be introduced in order to ensure that the low frequency impulses are kept within the limit of amplitude required for modulation. It is usual to divide this process into two stages, first a local amplifier situated close to the studio and second a control amplifier. The studio amplifier may consist of three or four stages of amplification and is similar in design and construction to the low frequency amplifiers which we have already discussed in connection with reception. It is more usual to employ resistance or choke coupled amplifiers because the minimum distortion is essential. The input to the amplifier is fed from a transformer having its primary winding connected across the microphone. The studio amplifier output is connected to the input of the second or control amplifier, which again may consist of three or four stages of resistance or choke coupled valves, but which incorporates high resistance potentiometers in the grid circuits of the first and second valves.

An operator is continually on duty at this amplifier, and, by manipulating the potentiometer, controls the amplitude of its output. For this purpose he employs visual and aural control, the former by means of a galvanometer calibrated so that the deflections of its needle coincide with those of a similar instrument in the amplifier at the transmitter, and the latter either by connecting a pair of telephones in a suitable position in the amplifier or else by connecting them to a wireless receiving apparatus which receives the transmission which he himself is actually controlling.

There are then three stages of amplification before the impulses generated by the microphone can be utilised for modulation.

MODULATION

Before examining the process of modulating the high frequency output of a radio telephony transmitter, the reader should cast his mind back to a discussion in an earlier chapter of this book connected with the transmission and reception of signals from a spark transmitter. (page 53). It will be remembered that the frequency at which oscillations were generated by the transmitter depended upon the characteristics and tuning of the oscillatory circuit of the transmitter, but that the frequency with which damped groups of high frequency waves were generated depended upon the rate of discharge of the spark gap. It will also be remembered that it was only by breaking up the high frequency oscillations into these groups that we were able to hear them in the telephones, because the latter would not respond to the frequency at which it was necessary to transmit the oscillations composing each group. Actually what took place was as follows.

On the application of a suitable voltage to the oscillatory circuit the condenser started to charge up, until the strain was so great between the two points of the spark gap that the insulation broke down and the condenser was discharged, only to charge up again and discharge once more in the other direction through the spark gap, and so on, each oscillation getting feebler and feebler in amplitude until the spark gap no longer broke down when another charge built up and the same process was repeated.

Obviously, then, the amplitude varies until it dies away, when the spark gap ceases to act as a conductor. If we were to express this graphically we should draw an ordinary sine wave expressing amplitude by the length which each half wave represented on either side of the centre zero line (as in Fig. 7). We may say then that it is the varying amplitude of the high frequency waves which breaks them up into groups, and because they are only audible when broken up into groups we can carry this logic further and say that it is the varying amplitude of the high frequency waves which renders them audible. We know that the frequency of the spark determines the note which is heard in the telephones at the receiving station, and it follows from this that the frequency of the change of the amplitude of the high frequency waves from one value through a greater or lesser value back to the same value determines the note heard in the telephones. It would seem therefore that all that would be required would be to vary the rate of discharge of a spark gap in synchrony with the varying frequencies of speech to achieve transmission of telephony. The idea is right, but it is impracticable, and we must find other means to work along the same lines. We must dispense with groups of high frequency waves and generate absolutely smooth continuous waves and find means whereby we can vary the amplitude in synchrony with the speech or music with which we desire to modulate the high frequency continuous waves.

Now turn to the explanation of the three-electrode valve as an oscillator, page 75, look at Fig. 19 and read the associated paragraphs. The valve oscillates because the grid is alternately positive and negative. The amplitude of the oscillations will depend primarily on the amount of current fed back to the grid from the anode circuit. Supposing that this is constant, the resultant oscillations are also constant, and we are generating continuous waves of equal amplitude. We should draw these graphically as a series of sine waves of which the peaks and troughs were all equidistant from the centre zero line. If we arrange the grid and anode coils so that the frequency of oscillation is one million per second, then the circuit will generate continuous waves of that frequency.

Now supposing that we introduce some means by which it is possible to vary the current fed back to the grid circuit, say, one thousand times per second, we could vary the amplitude of the continuous waves, so that instead of the peaks and troughs all being equidistant from the zero line they would take the form shown diagramatically in Fig. 39.

The continuous waves go on from the transmitter at the rate of a million a second, but the amplitude changes every one-thousandth of a second, so that the maximum amplitude is at the point A and, one-half cycle later, the minimum is at the point B, Fig. 39.   The outside lines of Fig. 39 representing the amplitude variations at a thousand

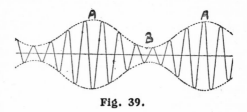

Fig. 39.

cycles are often referred to as the envelope of the carrier wave.

Now let us consider what takes place at the receiving end.   We know that the high frequency waves themselves cannot vibrate the diaphragm of the telephone receiver or loud speaker, but after rectification the latter will respond faithfully to the form of the envelope—that is to say, to the decrease and increase of amplitude of the high frequency waves, just in the same way as it responded to the commencement and conclusion of each group of damped waves from the spark transmitter.   Rectification must, of course, take place since the resultant average pulses must be unidirectional.   If there were no rectification the telephones would not respond even to the thousand cycle modulation frequency because each high frequency half-wave would oppose the preceding one and the diaphragm would remain stationary.

There is one important point which must be borne in mind. We must not confuse the continuous waves used to carry speech and music with the continuous wave which we receive as morse signals ; the latter, it must be remembered, have to be heterodyned at the receiving station before they are audible. For the reception of telephony no heterodyne is required ; if applied it will not only spoil the reception of the telephony but also interfere with the reception of other listeners in the vicinity. If the receiver incorporates some means of providing reaction, great care must be taken that this is not coupled up so tightly as to produce a heterodyne on the carrier wave.

In the case of telephony reception we do not want to hear the carrier wave, but only what it carries. Having grasped these elementary principles of telephony transmission and reception and seen how a continuous wave may be modulated so that it is audible without the application of a local heterodyne, we will consider the practical means by which the requisite variations of carrier wave amplitude are achieved.

The modulation of continuous waves may be achieved in a variety of different manners.

MODULATION BY ABSORPTION.

The simplest and most elementary method is that which is generally referred to as modulation by absorption. The continuous wave output of the oscillation generator is fed into an aerial system and a microphone is connected to that system, usually between the inductance and earth. When the microphone is not in use its resistance is constant and the circuit may be tuned to deliver continuous oscillations at the required frequency, the amount of high frequency current flowing in the aerial being dependent, of course, upon the voltage applied to the anode of the oscillator valve. The amplitude of the resultant continuous waves will be constant. When the microphone is actuated by speech, its resistance will, as we know, vary in synchrony with the sound frequencies, producing a variation of aerial current, which is the same thing as a variation of carrier wave amplitude. This method is only suitable when used with very low power transmitters such as might be used for a small portable set required to communicate between two points a few hundred yards apart. Furthermore, it is only suitable for the transmission of speech as apart from music, and even this will not be particularly good quality, though by careful adjustment average intelligibility can be achieved.

GRID MODULATION

Another method which can be applied to slightly more powerful transmitting stations is that which is termed "modulation by grid control." In this method modulation is achieved by exercising control over the actual oscillator valve. In this case the secondary of a transformer is introduced into the grid circuit, the primary being connected across a microphone. This arrangement is shown diagrammatically in Fig. 40. The valve is arranged as an oscillator similar to that shown in Fig. 19, except that the anode coil is directly coupled to the aerial coil, the two forming an auto-transformer. Now we know that the valve will oscillate continuously by reason of the impulses on the grid fed back to the grid coil from the anode coil. Supposing, then, that we set the valve to oscillate continuously at a frequency of 1,000,000 cycles per second (300 metres wavelength).

Every one millionth of a second the voltage on the grid is varying, arresting and assisting the flow of current through the valve, thus maintaining oscillation. The amplitude of these oscillations will depend, firstly, upon the voltage which is applied to the anode and, secondly, upon the induced voltage which is applied to the grid, consequently the current flowing in the aerial will depend also upon these two factors. If we leave the anode voltage exactly as it was and vary the grid voltage by some means, the aerial current must rise and fall with the variations of grid potential.

A glance at the diagram, Fig. 40, will show that the microphone and its associated transformer supply this need. Imagine that the microphone is suspended in front of a piano, and that we strike a note having a frequency of 1,000 cycles. Sound waves impinge on the microphone at the rate of 1,000 per second, creating variations of current in the microphone circuit through the primary of the transformer. These are induced in the secondary of the transformer, but the latter is connected

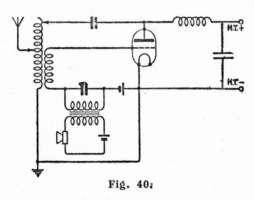

Fig. 40.

in the grid circuit of the valve, the voltage of which is already varying at the rate of a million times per second. The induced voltage in the secondary of the transformer will therefore be added to or subtracted from the existing grid voltage variations at the rate of a thousand times per second. Supposing that a state of affairs exists where the process of generating oscillations in the valve is at the point where the grid is at its maximum positive potential and is about to become less positive until it passes through zero and gradually reaches its maximum negative value. At the same moment the induced low frequency voltage variation from the microphone is at its maximum negative value and is about to alternate towards a positive value.

The negative low frequency voltage must be subtracted from the positive high frequency voltage, with the result that less positive is impressed on the grid of the valve than would be the case were there no variations due to the microphone. The result is to decrease the amplitude of the oscillations and consequently to decrease the current flowing in the aerial ; one half low frequency cycle later the opposite will obtain, and so on, the low frequency voltage variations adding to and subtracting from the total voltage applied to the grid of the valve, the result appearing in the form of current variations in the aerial having a frequency of a thousand cycles. In other words, the continuous wave output is modulated at a thousand cycles. This type of transmitter is suitable for medium powers and has been successfully used by amateur experimenters. It has obvious limitations, in that the degree of modulation which can be obtained by controlling the voltage of the grid is small.

The method is not suitable for broadcasting where higher powers are involved, but it has been used with considerable success for the commercial transmission of radio telephony, and in low power apparatus for intercommunication for short distances, such as are required for military and other purposes. The system normally employed for modulating the output of a broadcasting transmitter also relies for its action on controlling the oscillating valve, but at the anode and not at the grid.

Supposing we remove the microphone and transformer from the grid circuit of Fig. 40, place it in series with high tension supply, that is to say, between the right hand end of the air-cored choke (which incidentally is only there to prevent high frequency currents straying through the high tension supply) and the positive H.T. terminal, having of course closed the grid circuit where the secondary of the microphone transformer was.

Now when the microphone is actuated by speech varying voltages are induced in the secondary of the transformer. These are alternately added to and subtracted from the high tension voltage which is applied to the anode of the oscillator. If a thousand-cycle note were impressed upon the microphone, the total H.T. voltage applied to the anode of the oscillator would vary every one-thousandth of a second, with the consequence that the amplitude of the oscillations will vary and also the aerial current. In its simplest form this achieves modulation at the anode of the oscillator valve.

In itself this method is not practicable for broadcasting or for use with high powered transmitting apparatus, because the current variations which the sensitive microphone can produce in the secondary of the transformer are infinitesimal in relation to the power required to achieve transmission over any distance. To some extent this difficulty may be overcome by low frequency amplification. The microphone transformer, instead of being connected directly in the H.T. supply, may be connected to the input of a low frequency amplifier which can be designed to produce by progressive stages of amplification an output of much greater power. The output of this amplifier is connected to the high tension supply through a transformer, the secondary of which occupies the same position as did the secondary of the microphone transformer before the introduction of the low frequency amplifier. The valves of the low frequency amplifier may in this case be referred to as the " modulator " or " control " valve. This method, while effective to a certain degree, is not so efficient, practicable or economical as another method which is termed the " constant current " or " choke control method."

CHOKE MODULATION

This method is shown diagramatically in Fig. 41. V1 is an oscillator valve, V2 is the modulator or control valve. Ch. 1 is a high frequency choke whose function is to prevent the high frequency oscillations from the oscillator valve straying back into the modulator valve circuit and high tension supply. Ch. 2 is a speech choke.

This latter is wound in such a manner as to have an impedance so high as to afford practically a complete barrier to audible frequencies.

The microphone through its associated transformer is connected across the grid filament circuit of the modulator valve. When the microphone is idle the current from the H.T. supply is divided between the oscillator and modulator valves, since these two are connected in parallel. When the microphone is actuated by speech or music the anode current of the modulator valve varies in synchrony, but between the anode and the H.T. supply is the high impedance speech choke which refuses to allow variations

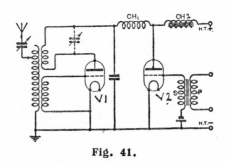

Fig. 41.

of current at any audible frequency to pass through it. So that the current supplied by the H.T. does not vary as the anode current of the modulator valve varies. Something. however, must supply the additional current for each positive impulse on the grid of the modulator valve and absorb the decreases of current with each negative swing. There is only one place where these changes can be taking place, and that is at the anode of the oscillator valve which, when the microphone was idle, shared the total current supply from the source of H.T. with the modulator valve.

It may be simpler to understand it if we put it another way. We will say for the sake of argument that the total current from the H.T. supply is 100 milliamps., which is absorbed equally at the rate of 50 milliamps. each between the oscillator and modulator valves. Supposing that when the grid of the modulator valve is at maximum negative due to the voltage variations of the microphone circuit,there is a decrease in its anode current of 25 milliamps. This decrease is absorbed by the oscillator valve and added to its normal anode current, so that its total at the same moment is 75 milliamps., the feed from the H.T. supply remaining constant at 100 milliamps.

Conversely, when a half cycle later the grid of the modulator valve is at maximum positive, 75 milliamps. will flow in the anode of that valve and only 25 in the anode of the oscillator, the current from the high tension supply still remaining constant at 100 milliamps. Thus with each increase of anode current in the modulator valve there is an exactly corresponding decrease in the oscillator valve resulting in a decrease of aerial current and vice versa. It must be understood that the figures given above for anode currents are purely hypothetical, and are used for simple illustration only.

The transmitting apparatus described above forms the basis of the majority of broadcasting transmitters in use to-day. Of course, where high powers are involved it is necessary to apply the microphone voltage variations to the grid filament circuit of the modulator valve through a low-frequency control amplifier, or a series of amplifiers, instead of direct through a transformer. The prime necessity is that the degree of control which the modulator valve exercises upon the oscillations generated by the oscillator valve should be in correct proportion of the carrier wave amplitude. Whatever degree of amplification is necessary the amplifiers must be so designed as to insure an equal degree of modulation at all frequencies within a range of 50-10,000 cycles for a given input voltage variation.

In the type of transmitter which we have been considering this, of course, resolves itself only into a question of correct design of low-frequency amplifiers, and the problem is almost exactly the same as that which we discussed in connection with the low-frequency amplifiers used in receiving apparatus.

As this book is written for the listener and not for the experimental transmitter, it would be beyond its scope to go more deeply into the question of the cause and effect of over or under-modulation. All we want is a rough idea of what happens in the transmitter, in order that we may understand the action of the receiving circuits.

CHAPTER VIII

RECEPTION OF WIRELESS TELEPHONY

BEFORE we discussed transmitters we sketched a very brief outline of the part played by the receiver of modulated continuous waves. Now we must go a little more fully into the matter.

An interested friend to whom the writer is indebted has asked for an explanation in the form of several questions which, he says, no writer has explained satisfactorily. This is a sweeping statement, but the author will do his best. It will perhaps be best to explain the action of the receiver by replying to each of his questions in turn. His first is : " Exactly what happens to waves and undulations as they pass through our sets and on to the 'phones ? " He strikes a fundamental note in this question, and in its briefest form the answer is that the waves (by which it is presumed that he means the high-frequency carrier waves) do not pass through the receiver or telephones, but the modulations do. Let us try and apply an analogy. Examined under a microscope it would be found that the surface of the metal composing a rail on the permanent way of a railway track is by no means the flat surface which it appears to the naked eye. It is anything but flat, and would be seen to consist of thousands of indentations and excrescences. A wheel of an express train travelling over this rail does not record the vibrations due to this unevenness of the surface of the rail, and the passenger in the coach above has the sensation of travelling along a perfectly flat surface, although the wheel is actually striking several thousand excrescences a second. The rail, then, is analogous to the carrier wave, but let the rail rise and fall one foot in every ten of its length, and the passenger will most certainly be aware of the result. But here is the important point. It is not the thousands of little unevennesses of the rail itself that he feels, but the undulations of the rail as a whole. The analogy is not a good one—analogies seldom are—but it may help.

The transmitter is tuned to emit carrier waves at a frequency of, say, 1,000,000 cycles (300 metres). We modulate it with a 1,000-cycle note. We may say that as the carrier wave frequency is a million and the

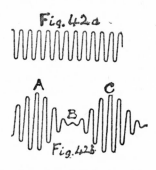

Fig. 42a

Fig. 42b

modulation wave is a thousand cycles, a complete modulation cycle will consist of a thousand undulations of the carrier wave. If the modulation is complete— that is to say, at the minimum point the amplitude of the carrier wave is zero—then this point must be the five-hundredth carrier wave oscillation, and at the thousandth the amplitude will again be at maximum. Now just as the vast number of small indentations and excrescences on the rail fail to produce any sensation to the passenger, so are the high frequency waves inaudible ; but if we make a continuous stream of these high frequency waves wobble up and down by varying their amplitude at an audible frequency, the wobble is audible. Look at the diagram (Fig. 42b). It is, of course, impossible to show enough waves diagrammatically to give an exact mathematical representation of waves of a frequency of a million cycles modulated at a frequency of a thousand. But assume that there are a thousand waves between points A and C, then the point B will be the five-hundredth wave. A curve joining together A, B, C would, of course, represent one cycle of the modulation frequency. Diagram 42a shows the same carrier wave before modulation commences.

The important thing to remember is that the carrier wave goes on and its frequency never alters ; it is only its amplitude which alters. The railway track has the same unevenness of surface throughout its length, but it was the variation of the level of the track which produced the effect on the passenger in the coach.

Fig. 42b represents the form in which the modulated carrier wave arrives at the receiver. Alternating current having a frequency of a million cycles is set up in the receiving aerial—that is to say, electrons start to rush backward and forward along and around it, but the strength at which they rush backward and forward is varied a thousand times a second.

We have discussed the form of the modulated carrier wave as it reaches the aerial at the receiving station and discovered that the carrier wave is only a means to an end. We only want it because it is impossible to radiate electromagnetic waves at any but a very high frequency in relation to that band of frequencies which falls within the audible limit. The high frequency waves are, themselves, inaudible because even if we rectify them and turn them into unidirectional currents of the same frequency the diaphragm of the telephone is physically incapable of vibrating so rapidly, and, if it were capable, the human ear would not be able to detect the resultant sound waves. But the high frequency waves must nevertheless be rectified in order that the resultant pulses of low frequency unidirectional current may operate the telephone diaphragm. Rectification, then, is the first thing that " happens to the waves as they pass through our sets." Turn back to Fig. 42b, and you will see a modulated carrier wave in diagrammatic form. Supposing that we did not rectify these waves, what would happen ? We should try and pass an alternnating current of a frequency of 1,000,000 cycles through the telephones, and even though this current varied in amplitude a thousand times a second (or at any other modulation frequency), we should hear nothing because each successive half-wave would start to push the telephone diaphragm away from the magnet before it had had time to bend towards it in response to the preceding half-wave. It would make no difference at all that the amplitude of the alterations happened to be varying at the frequency of modulation, because, no matter what the strength of each half-wave might be, its effect on the telephone diaphragm would still be reversed by the half-wave immediately following which has (*vide* Fig. 42b) virtually the same strength. But if we remove this second half-wave by putting a barrier in its way so that it can never reach the telephone coil, the diaphragm is free to vibrate, in synchrony with the amplitude variations. Any form of rectifier, either a crystal or a valve, affords such a barrier. In the case of the crystal, only one half-wave can pass through into the telephone circuit because a crystal can only pass current in one direction. In the case of a valve arranged as a " bottom-bend " rectifier the same thing occurs by a different method. The first half-wave, we will say, for example, is positive ; there is an increase of anode current as the grid becomes positive. The next half-wave is negative and the flow of anode current is arrested. The amount of positive potential applied to the grid controls the extent to which the anode current will increase. If the modulation frequency is 1,000 cycles and the carrier frequency is 1,000,000 cycles, and if the first half-wave to arrive at the grid has the maximum positive value, the succeeding half-waves will be gradually less positive until, at the five-hundredth, the potential is minimum, rising to maximum again at the one-thousandth. Thus there is a rise and fall of anode current in response to the modulation frequency. Now this is all we want : the carrier wave has done its job, it has carried the modulation frequency (in the form of variations in its own amplitude) to the rectifier valve, where it is faithfully recorded in the low frequency fluctuation of anode current. The high frequency fluctuations of anode current due to the rectified half-waves of the carrier wave are now of no further use to us and can be dispensed with. This is accomplished by providing them with a path to earth through a condenser having a very low resistance to their frequency and a very high resistance to the low frequency fluctuations. Thus the modulation frequency only is passed on the telephone or amplifier, and the carrier wave, having served its purpose, is dispensed with.

" Why is it always said that only the detector valve rectifies, though every valve must do so or it would not be a valve ? " This is the question which has been addressed to us.

It is evident at the outset that he has misunderstood the uses to which the three-electrode valve may be put, and has not appreciated the fact that the valve operates in an entirely different manner for each of these uses. If the reader will cast his mind back, he will remember that in discussing the three-electrode valve we came to the conclusion that it had three main uses. Firstly we discussed its use as an oscillator which has been dealt with elsewhere, and we are not now concerned with it, or should not be, since it is the duty of every listener in operating his broad-cast receiver to ensure that the valves do not oscillate. However, there is one material point bearing upon our correspondent's query. He infers that a valve must rectify whatever the use to which it is put, or else it is not a valve. We can dispose of this suggestion at once by going back to the point where we discussed the operation of the three-electrode valve as an oscillator and learnt that so far from being an essential rectifier the valve can, when properly connected and adjusted, do precisely the opposite, that is to say, convert a direct current into an alternating one.

Secondly, we discussed the valve as a rectifier, and considered the principles and means by which it can be made to achieve the desired results. We have

considered more closely and in greater detail the part
played by the rectifier valve in the reception of
modulated continuous waves, that is to say, in the
reception of radio telephony. We have seen how the
rectifier cuts off every other half-cycle of the carrier
wave and registers the variations of carrier wave
amplitude, in the form of variations of its own
anode current. Having recorded these variations of
amplitude the carrier wave is of no use, and is by-passed
to earth, the resultant anode current variations being left
behind either to operate telephones or to be amplified.
Now this is where, we think, our correspondent's difficulty
really begins, namely, in the third use of the valve, which
is amplification. He seems to be under the impression
that a valve arranged as an amplifier must rectify the varying currents which pass through it, but just as the oscillator

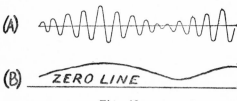

Fig. 43.

valve could be arranged so that it did the reverse of
rectification, so can the amplifier valve be arranged so
that rectification is avoided. There are, of course, two
entirely different methods of amplification, namely,
high-frequency amplification and low-frequency amplification. It would be better to treat the latter first, since
if falls in a more logical sequence on what we have been
discussing.

To understand the reason why the amplifier valve does
not rectify, we must revert for a moment to the rectifier
valve and consider the form of the current flowing in its
anode circuit. We know that the carrier wave arrives in
the receiving aerial in the form shown diagrammatically

in Fig. 43 (A), which represents high frequency waves modulated at an audible frequency. Now, if these waves were not modulated every one would be of equal size in the diagram. We can see from the diagram that the modulation is taking place because of the difference in amplitude which is illustrated by the varying depth of the waves through the zero line from peak to trough. Now the detector does its work, and everything below the zero line in Fig. 43 (A) disapppears, and we have left only the half cycles above the zero line. This then is the form of the detector anode current, which you may see as a diagram by taking a sheet of paper and laying it across the page so that its upper edge coincides with the zero line of Fig. 43 (A). It is obvious that it is no longer truly an alternating current, because it does not completely change its phase. It is rather unidirectional pulses all on one side of the zero line, that is to say, each successive pulse is travelling in the same direction, and there are none travelling in the opposite direction. If we should wish to show a curve representing the variations of amplitude due to modulation, the way to accomplish this would be to join up the peaks. Now, we have done with the carrier wave, and we give it a decent burial through a condenser to earth. The amplitude variations cannot go the same way, however much they want to, because of the resistance of the condenser to their particular frequency; therefore they get left behind in the anode circuit and have the form shown diagrammatically in Fig. 43 (B), which is nothing more nor less than a series of curves plotting the points where the peaks of the high frequency unidirectional pulses were before their departure *via* the by-pass condenser to earth. We now have continuous unidirectional current varying in amplitude on one side of the zero line, and which will continue for so long as modulation is sustained by the transmitter. This is the important point, that what is left is only *variation of the amplitude of a continuous current* and is *not* in the true sense an alternating current, therefore there is no inducement to the next low-frequency amplifier valve to rectify.

If properly arranged the variations of amplitude will be impressed in the form of amplified voltage variations on the grid of this amplifier valve (page 68) producing exactly similar, but amplified variations in its anode current to those which are flowing in the detector anode, *vide* Fig. 43 (B). The only condition under which there will be any tendency for the amplifier valve to rectify is if so much negative grid bias is applied as to cause cut-off of part of the lower portions of the wave form of Fig. 43 (B).

The reader should now be fully acquainted with the conditions under which low-frequency amplification takes place without rectification. Of course, a low-frequency amplifier valve may rectify under certain conditions. If the wrong type of valve is selected—say one with a very close mesh grid—it is possible for part of the wave form, illustrated in Fig. 43 (B), to be suppressed. This, however, is improbable, since the manufacturers of modern valves give adequate instruction and clear markings on the valve itself as well as on the carton in which it is packed to indicate its correct position in the set and the approximate operating conditions.

Another cause which is much more likely to give rise to rectification or partial rectification by a low-frequency valve is the application of too much negative to the grid. A certain negative-potential is required on the grid of any low-frequency amplifying valve in order that the valve may operate on the most advantageous part of its characteristic curve. Since the object is to obtain the maximum *variation* of anode current for a given change of grid volts it is obvious that the straight, nearly vertical part of the curve is the part we want. We want to avoid the part where the curve starts to become horizontal at the top, because in that direction lies the saturation point and obviously a large change of grid volts would only produce a small change in anode current. Conversely we must avoid the flat-bottom bend of the curve because rectification takes place there. Look at Fig. 16, on page 68. It is

what is known as the " grid volt-anode current characteristic curve " of a typical three-electrode valve plotted for
three different values of anode voltage.   The top portion
of the curve must be avoided because it flattens out towards
saturation, and the positive grid swings or upper portion
of the wave form, Fig. 43 (B), will produce relatively no

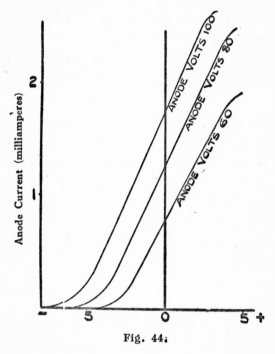

Fig. 44.

increase in anode current.   The lower bend must also be
avoided because the lower portion of the wave form will
have virtually no effect on the anode current and may even
arrest it altogether.   As the grid voltage is amplified from
stage to stage of the low-frequency amplifier it becomes
necessary to apply more auxiliary negative or " biasing "

potential to the grid to pull the anode current down out of the upper danger zone ; but if we put more negative on the grid than is required for this purpose, we shall find ourselves trying to operate the valve in the other danger zone, where rectification or partial rectification of the low-frequency pulses may take place. In passing it may be remembered that as much negative should always be applied to the grid of a low-frequency amplifying valve as is possible without coming too near the danger zone of rectification. This is advisable in order to reduce to an economic minimum the current drawn from the source of anode voltage. A glance at the left-hand curve of Fig. 16 will show that the same *rise* in anode current is obtained for an increase of 3.5 grid volts from— 4 to —0.5 as will be produced by the same increase from —2.5 volts to +1 volt, but in the first case the current from the source of anode volts is only 0.5 to 1.5 milliamps and in the second is from 1 to 2 milliamps. Therefore, if we apply 1.5 volts negative to the grid in the second case we achieve the same result and economise to the extent of $\frac{1}{2}$ milliampere from the anode battery. Of course, these figures will be very much higher when the argument is applied to the last valve of an amplifier which may be of a type which can and will handle an anode current of 15 milliamps. Our object in amplification is to achieve the *maximum change of anode current for a given change of grid volts* and *not* to see how much anode current we can make a certain grid voltage produce. We have, then, got so far in answering our correspondent's question as to dispose of the suggestion that a low frequency amplifying valve *must* rectify. Now what about the high frequency valve ? Why does it not rectify ? The problem is very much the same only rather easier. It is almost entirely a question of selecting the right type of valve and operating it on the proper part of its characteristic curve where there is no danger of the negative half cycles producing a state of affairs where the anode current becomes zero. The problem is easier because even if a high frequency valve does rectify to some small extent it doesn't greatly matter, because the rectifier is going to remove half the complete wave anyhow.

Now we come to the next question which our friend has addressed to us. Paraphrased, it is as follows : " If the half-wave which is left by the detector valve goes through a transformer, what good has been done by cutting the wave in half, for presumably the resulting alternations should have the same mutually neutralising effect as regards the telephones as the two halves of the complete wave would have had ? "

In the main this question has already been answered by our recent discussion of the form of the modulated high-frequency currents in the anode circuit of the rectifier valve. We know that the high frequency component is by-passed to earth and therefore does not come into the question at all so far as the transformer is concerned. The only fluctuation of current which passes through the primary winding of the transformer (it is assumed that it is a low frequency transformer with its primary connected in the anode circuit of the rectifier valve to which our correspondent refers) is that which is due to the varying grid voltage of the detector valve produced by the varying amplitude of the carrier wave itself—*i.e.* modulation. But what is clear from our correspondent's question is that he has not appreciated the action of the transformer, which is based on the elementary principles of magnetic induction.

In a very early chapter of this book we discussed induced currents and observed, in making the process of induction clear, that induced current in a circuit flows in the opposite direction to that which is flowing in the circuit from which it was induced. While this is actually true, it might have been expressed in another way by saying that when the current is rising in the primary it is falling in the secondary, and *vice versa.* Our friend evidently imagines that because the current flows in the opposite direction in the secondary of the transformer to that of the primary, the result is to replace the half-cycle which has been suppressed in the rectifier valve. Of course this is obviously impossible. In the first place the half-cycles of high-frequency current

L

which do pass through the detector valve are by-passed
to earth before they get to the primary of the transformer,
and even if they did pass through the transformer the fact
that their direction is reversed in the secondary does
not mean that the complete wave is restored. We know
that the only current passing through the transformer
is that which we showed in Fig. 43B (page 156). Admittedly
this is not truly an alternating current, but it is a fluctuating
current, and as such is just as effective from the induction
point of view. The form of the current flowing in the
secondary will be precisely the same as that flowing in the
primary, albeit it will be of opposite phase at any given
moment. There is no question of restoring any part of a
wave form which may have been suppressed at an earlier
stage.

We have now dealt with the salient questions raised
by our friend. Certain minor points which he raised
have been covered by the answers to the main questions.
There is one question which purposely we have not dealt
with. He asks, " If the function of the rectifier is to cut
off half the high frequency wave, would it be possible to
dispense with a rectifier if the B.B.C. sent out only one-
half of the wave ? " We cannot go into a very deep
discussion on this point because it would involve us in
certain details of radiation which are of a very highly
technical nature and which cannot be comprehended
without reference to matters outside the scope of this book.
Suffice it to say that the answer to the question is emphati-
cally " No," and the reason is that it is not feasible from
the broadcasting point of view. We must modify this
assertion by remarking that there is a process of transmitting
telephony by a system which relies for its action on the
partial suppression of the carrier wave. We need not discuss
this system in detail because it cannot in its present stage
of development be applied to broadcasting. It does not,
however, render a rectifier an unnecessary part of the
apparatus required for its reception.

Having acquired a working knowledge of the transmission
and reception of radio telephony, we have come within
sight of the object we set out to achieve. Before closing

this book, however, the discussion of some subsidiary subjects will be of value to the reader. For instance, it will no doubt be helpful to have some knowledge of the construction and proper operation of the storage batteries required for receiving apparatus rectifying and smoothing apparatus required for operating a set from the electric light mains. These and similar matters will be discussed in the last chapter.

CHAPTER IX

ANCILLARY APPARATUS.

Telephones and Loud Speakers—Accumulators—High Ten-
sion Batteries—High Tension from the Mains.

TELEPHONES AND LOUD SPEAKERS

ONE is accustomed to allude to the telephone or the
loud speaker as a "Receiver." This probably
originates from the ordinary land line telephone
where the actual ear-piece is, in fact, a receiver. In the
case of wireless, the telephone or loud speaker is merely
an accessory after the fact. "Reception" has to be accomplished first, and then the signal rendered audible by the
telephones or loud speaker. In our earlier studies we
considered the essential components of a telephone ear-
piece. These, it will be remembered, consist of a U-
shaped magnet having an inductance coil wound round
each arm of the U. Suspended above the magnet
in a horizontal plane is a thin iron diaphragm. When
the low frequency pulses of rectified current pass through
the inductance coils which are connected together in
series the magnet attracts and releases the diaphragm
in synchrony with the incoming signal. Each backward
and forward movement of the diaphragm displaces a
quantity of air and gives rise to an air wave. It is just
the same thing as our old friend the stone, dropped into
the pond. The air waves impinge upon the delicate
mechanism of the listener's ear (far more delicately and
intricately made than the clumsy man-made magnetic

telephone), and set up vibration of its diaphragm. Air waves like wireless waves travel in all directions at the same time. Their rate of travel is 1,100 feet per second, very slow in relation to the 186,000 miles per second at which wireless waves travel.

Naturally, the greater the amount of air displaced with each vibration of the diaphragm the greater will be the amplitude of the air wave, that is to say, the louder will be the sound.

An iron diaphragm such as is used in an ordinary telephone ear-piece displaces only a small mass of air with each vibration and has consequently to be held close to the listener's ear in order that the resultant sound may be heard.

If, however, a column of air is enclosed in a trumpet-shaped horn and the diaphragm attached to the small end, each vibration will displace the whole of the air column within the horn, with the result that the effective volume of sound will be enormously increased. As well as increasing the sound, however, this arrangement will also project the sound waves directionally to some extent.

The ordinary megaphone used to address a large crowd in an open space is a good example of the directional projection of sound waves. Standing behind the user less can be heard than if he had no megaphone, but in front of him his words are heard much more loudly and to a much greater distance. The same principle may be applied to any source of sound waves ; consequently the most elementary form of loud speaker may consist of a telephone ear-piece such as has been described attached to some form of horn.

Although by far the greater number of loud speakers in use in England to-day consist of a metal diaphragm and horn, this arrangement is far from ideal. In the first place the diaphragm has one or more mechanical resonance frequencies, which will introduce distortion although the air column in the horn will, if the latter is carefully designed, offer sufficient damping effect to counteract this to some extent. Secondly, it is extremely difficult to design a diaphragm which is capable of moving through the larger distance required for a low frequency with as much force as at a higher one ; consequently the lower frequencies of the musical scale are not reproduced at their proper value and some are not reproduced at all.

The ordinary horn loud speaker does not reproduce faithfully below about 200 cycles. Again, a note of high frequency which is superimposed on a note of lower frequency may not be truthfully reproduced because the diaphragm will not be the same average distance from the magnet during the whole of the time for which the high frequency note is sustained because it is moving in response to the lower frequency at the same time. The resonance effects of the horn itself are also detrimental to faithful reproduction.

What has come to be known as the cone type of loud speaker gets over some of the difficulties of the horn type. The mechanism consists of much the same components as the horn type, with the important exception that the metal diaphragm is replaced by a small steel armature held above the ends of coil wound magnet. Attached to the armature is some form of reed generally consisting of a piece of thin steel rod to which is attached a conical paper diaphragm of large diameter. The advantages of this type over the horn type are that the resonant frequency of the diaphragm will be very low, that the larger diameter of the diaphragm will furnish greater movement in response to the lower frequencies, that the horn and its resonance effects are eliminated, as the air displacement of the larger diameter diaphragm is sufficient without the aid of an air column.

The latest development of loud speaker design also employs a conical paper diaphragm, but operates on a somewhat different principle. A large permanent or electro-magnet is held rigidly in a frame. The magnet is in the form of an enclosed cylinder having a central core.

A small circular gap is left between the central core and the end of the magnet. If the latter is to be an electro-magnet the core is wound with a suitable coil the ends of which are attached to a source of E.M.F. In the air gap between the core and the outer shell of the magnet is suspended a coil wound on a cylindrical former. The coil former is rigidly attached to the apex of a paper cone, the outer periphery of the cone is suspended either by sheet rubber or by thin leather or other resilient substance to the same rigid frame as holds the magnet. The received signal is passed through the coil, causing it to move back and forth in the field of magnet, air being displaced with each movement by the cone.

The chief advantages of this arrangement over the cone and horn loud speakers are that the method of construction allows the coil to move through the large distances requisite to the reproduction of low frequencies, that the influence of the magnet on the coil is sensibly the same whatever position the coil may be in in the course of a vibration. That the resonant frequencies of the component parts of the loud speaker are very low and may usually be reduced to a value which is below the audible limit.

With this type of loud speaker it is usual to attach a flat " baffle " in the same plane as the cone, with the object of arresting the tendency of the lower frequencies to slip round to the back of the cone and neutralise themselves.

ACCUMULATOR BATTERIES

The accumulator, or, as it is sometimes called, the secondary battery, consists of two " active materials " as they are called immersed in an acid solution. The positive active material consists of lead peroxide and the negative of porous lead. The chemical solution consists of sulphuric acid diluted with distilled water.

The secondary battery can function in either of two directions, that is to say it can be discharged, or it can be charged. It can absorb or give out energy. The solution of sulphuric acid normally consists of about three parts of distilled water to one of sulphuric acid, giving a specific gravity of approximately 1.2.

In a cell as above described there is a difference in potential when fully charged of just over 2 volts between the positive and negative terminals. If the two terminals are joined together through a circuit having a certain resistance, steady current will flow round the circuit. The time for which this current will continue to flow will depend upon the area of active material which is immersed in the solution and upon the specific gravity of the solution.

IONIC ACTION OF THE CELL

Very early in our studies we learnt that the fundamental process of the flow of electrical current was the liberation of electrons which had been held separate from their positive nuclei. The function of the storage battery is to hold the electrons separated from their nuclei in a condition in which they can be readily released to respond to the attraction of the nuclei. Before a current passes through a cell, whether it is charging or discharging, it is assumed that the atoms of the acid solution are broken up into negative electrons and positive nuclei. When a current passes through the battery the electrons are attracted to the positive element and the positive nuclei to the negative element, so that there are two currents flowing in the opposite direction through the solution.

CHEMICAL ACTION OF THE CELL

Roughly, the chemical action is as follows :—Before commencing to discharge the cell, that is to say before connecting the two terminals together through the associated circuit, the positive active material consists of lead peroxide and the negative active material consists of porous lead. When the discharge commences the positive active material gives off oxygen which, in combination with the sulphuric acid of the solution forms a lead sulphate. While this is going on the porous lead of the negative active material also forms a lead sulphate by combination with the acid solution. The oxygen released from the positive element mixing with the hydrogen in the sulphuric acid solution produces water, with the result that the specific gravity, of the " electrolyte," as the acid solution is termed, falls. This fall in specific gravity, combined with the fact that both the elements are being slowly converted into lead sulphate, produces a corresponding fall in potential across the terminals of the battery. If now the circuit through which the cell was being discharged is removed, and a source of electrical current flowing in the opposite direction is connected in its place, the lead sulphate, which has been created on the positive and negative elements, is reconverted into lead peroxide and porous lead respectively, with the result that the specific gravity of the cell rises again to its normal value. When the cell reassumes its normal condition and no further rise of specific gravity takes place, it is said to be fully charged, and the positive and negative elements will be found to consist of their original substances, namely, lead peroxide and porous lead. At this point in the process of recharging it will be observed that bubbles of gas rise in the electrolyte. This is due to the fact that the applied current having restored the elements to their original state uses up its energy to break up the water which has been formed in the process of discharge. The above is a very brief outline of what takes place in charging and discharging a cell of an accumulator battery.

CAPACITY OF A CELL

The capacity of a cell, that is to say, the amount of electrical energy which it will store as a result of being charged, and which is available for discharge depends upon the area of active material which is immersed in the solution. It is calculated and referred to in terms of " ampère-hours," indicating the time for which a current can be maintained at a given rate of flow, that is to say a cell which is said to have a capacity of 60 ampère hours could maintain a current of one-ampère for 60 hours, or a current of 2 ampères for 30 hours before the voltage began to fall below 2 volts. The capacity of a cell, however, cannot be calculated as a direct progression because of a factor usually referred to as the rate of discharge. With the increased rate of discharge above a certain prescribed limit, the capacity will fall. The proper discharge rate will generally be found among the instructions printed on the side of the battery by the manufacturer, and in no circumstances should a battery be operated under conditions which exceed the discharge rate specified.

CONSTRUCTION OF A CELL

The active materials of a cell are attached to the surface of the plate by various means with which we are not here concerned. In a small cell of a limited capacity there might be only one positive plate and one negative plate, that is to say one plate coated with lead peroxide and one with porous lead. If a greater capacity is required a larger number of plates must be employed. The normal arrangement is to place the plates alternately, first a positive then a negative, and so on, joining all the positives and all the negatives together and attaching each group to its appropriate terminal, the container of the whole cell being so designed that the electrolyte will cover the whole of the surface of each plate.

From this very brief theoretical outline of the action of the electrolytic cell we will proceed to some practical considerations with regard to the proper operation and maintenance of accumulator batteries.

The proper care and maintenance of accumulator batteries requires no particular technical knowledge, and is in itself a simple matter providing that certain precautions are taken against the diseases which assail batteries of this nature.

The most common complaints from which accumulators suffer are the following :—sulphating, misshapen plates, short circuit due to the introduction of some foreign

body or a particle of active material falling between the
positive and negative plate, internal discharge, the
separation of the active material from its supporting
lead plate.

Let us examine in turn the indications, causes and
remedies of each of these troubles. The circumstances
which may cause sulphating are—discharging the accumulator beyond the point where the voltage begins to fall
rapidly, short circuiting, allowing the battery to remain
unused and in an uncharged condition for any considerable length of time, allowing the acid solution to fall to
too low a specific gravity, or the introduction of impurities
in the acid or distilled water used to compose the
solution.

When an accumulator is completely discharged, all the
active material on the positive plate, which, incidentally,
is of a brown colour as opposed to the grey colour
of the negative plate, becomes sulphate of lead. If it
is allowed to remain in this condition, the sulphate
of lead will turn into a hard and insoluble substance
which cannot be removed as can the normal sulphate
of lead resulting from a normal discharge. The
formation of this substance is referred to as " sulphating." This must not be confused with the normal
formation of sulphate of lead and consequent reversion to lead peroxide which takes place with discharge
and charge under healthy conditions. The presence
of sulphate in a cell is indicated by white spots on
the plates. In extreme cases it may take the form
of a white substance between the plates. If the
container of the cell is not transparent and does not therefore permit of the white sulphate spots being observed,
the condition can be recognised by a fall in the normal
capacity of the battery, overheating on discharge and
general inefficiency.

As regards remedies. If sulphating is taken in time,
when it is only slight, it may be remedied by a series of
long charges at a low rate. The normal rate at which
a healthy battery should be charged is one-tenth of its
ampère hour capacity. It may be as well to mention

at this point that some manufacturers of accumulator batteries indicate two capacities in the instructions on the side of the battery or accompanying it. One is the rate of intermittent discharge and the other the rate of constant discharge. Intermittent discharge generally means the use of the battery for such purposes as supplying the spark for an internal combustion engine when the circuit is closed intermittently by a rotating commutator. In our study of batteries as applied to wireless receivers, we are not concerned with anything but the constant discharge of the battery. The ampère hour capacity on constant discharge is generally half that of intermittent discharge. The capacity at constant discharge is sometimes referred to as the " actual capacity." The rate at which a sulphated battery should be charged as a curative measure may be a twentieth or less of the actual ampère hour capacity. The above remarks refer only to internal sulphating on and between the plates. Sulphating of the external terminals and links of the battery may also take place. This is generally due to a film of the acid solution becoming deposited on the top of the container and therefore in contact with the terminals. Care should therefore be taken not to allow the acid or distilled water to slop over when filling the battery, and to prevent violent gassing when charging, which may cause particles of solution to be shot up through the vent holes on to the top of the container. This external sulphating is not serious and can be easily remedied by carefully cleaning and smearing the terminals and links with vaseline.

The plates which contain the active material are formed of thin sheet lead. Lead is a substance which has no elasticity, and consequently if once bent does not reassume its normal shape. The chemical action which we have previously described is accompanied by the generation of heat. If this chemical action becomes uneven over the surface of the plate, it will tend to misshape the plate, due to greater expansion at one point than another. When a battery is discharged, the active material expands in the process of becoming sulphate of lead. This expansion

causes pressure on the lead plate to which the active
material is attached, and if discharge is too prolonged or
is uneven over the surface of the plate, may cause it to
buckle or even break. The formation of sulphate on a
plate will cause an uneven distribution of heat because
the hard sulphate has no conductivity and is in fact an
insulator. Even at low rates of discharge, a battery
which is badly sulphated may cause buckling on the plates.
Where no sulphate is present, the chief causes of misshapen plates are excessive discharge or too long a discharge
at the normal rate. Excessive rate of charging may
similarly cause buckling of the plates because when the
cell is being charged the acid generated at the surfaces of
the plates mixes with the water which was formed on
discharge and heat is generated. If the rate of charge is
too high or charging is prolonged beyond the point where
the battery is fully charged heat may develop such proportions as to cause warping of the plates. The buckling
in itself does not impede the ordinary action of the cell
but it tends to loosen the hold of the active material on
the surface of the lead plates which will tend to reduce
the capacity of the cell and may cause short circuiting
by pieces of active material falling from the surface of the
plate and becoming wedged between a positive and negative plate. If buckling is excessive it may cause the
plates actually to touch one another and set up short
circuit.

The remedy is beyond the capabilities of the ordinary
amateur : it is a case for the reconditioning of the battery
by the manufacturer since it entails dismantling, straight-
ening of the plates and replacement of the active material.

Now we come to short-circuiting. By this is meant,
of course, the short-circuiting due to some internal cause
in the battery, and not due to the careless or accidental
connection of the two terminals of the battery from
outside. The most frequent causes of short-circuiting
within the cell are either severe sulphating, buckling of
the plates, or fall of active material from the surface of
the plate. In the case of sulphating, it may be caused by
particles of hard sulphate becoming detached from the

lead supporting plate and falling between the positive and negative plate, or by a growth of sulphate building up to such an extent on one plate as to bridge the distance between it and its opposite plate. Another, but less frequent, cause of short-circuiting may be the introduction of impurities in the electrolyte or water. The remedies depend to some extent on the cause. If the cause is very severe sulphating, then the remedy appropriate to that ailment should be applied, but it is seldom effective if the short circuit is caused by a growth of sulphate bridging the two opposite plates, since in that case sulphating has probably gone too far. In the case of cells having a celluloid or other transparent container, short circuits due to causes other than sulphating may be seen and can be removed by passing a strip of wood or ebonite through the plates and pushing the obstruction down to the bottom of the cell below the level of the bottom of the plates. Sometimes, however, there is so much " sludge " in the bottom of the cell as to constitute in itself a source of short-circuiting. The sludge generally consists of lost active material from the surface of the plates caused by rough handling of the cell. In this case, the only remedy is to clean out the cell thoroughly at once. This is best done in the following manner : Empty the electrolyte from the cell and fill with pure distilled water. Rinse thoroughly, empty and fill again with pure distilled water. Repeat this operation three or four times until all sludge is removed from the bottom of the cell, then refill with acid solution of a specific gravity of approximately 1. 2. Recharge the cell at the normal rate.

The chief causes of loss of active material in a cell are sulphating, rough treatment and excessive gassing on account of too long or too high a rate of charging. In the latter case the bubbling of the water being driven from the cell in the form of gas may set up so great a vibration as to cause the active material to be shaken from the plate. There is no remedy which can be applied in the home. The battery must be returned to the manufacturer for the plates to be recoated with active material. It will generally be found that the loss of active material is more severe from the brown positive than from the grey negative plate.

Internal discharge is really nothing more or less than short-circuiting, but is mentioned as a separate ailment because it need not necessarily be due to the presence of some substance between the plates. If impurities are allowed to be introduced to the cell, or the plates of the cell, they may not actually cause a physical short circuit, but they may lead to internal discharge on account of chemical action.

The following are some general hints for the care and maintenance of batteries which should be observed. If, after being fully charged, the specific gravity of the electrolyte of a cell is below that specified in the manufacturers' instructions, a quantity of electrolyte should be withdrawn and acid of a specific gravity of about 1.5 substituted. The cell must then be recharged in order to allow the new acid to mix with the old electrolyte. Test half-an-hour after recharging and, if necessary, repeat the process until the specific gravity reading is correct. To test the specific gravity of a cell the reader should provide himself with a hydrometer. There is no need to describe this piece of apparatus. Its working is extremely simple. If the batteries are not charged in the home and are taken to a local charging station, it is as well to test them with a hydrometer before taking them away to see that the specific gravity is up to the full. To test with a voltmeter without the cell being under load means really nothing. To test the voltage, connect the battery to the set switch on the valves and then take a reading with a voltmeter. If the battery consists of two or more cells connected in series and shows symptoms of some ailment, test each cell separately with a voltmeter and hydrometer. If it is found that one cell has a short circuit, cut it out of the battery before charging. It is quite useless to charge a battery of several cells if one of them is faulty, and may do considerable harm to the other cells on account of overcharging. Do not treat you battery as a unit, remember that the unit is the cell, and give each unit individual attention. Batteries must always be charged at a higher voltage than the fully-charged voltage of the cell, that is to say, a battery consisting of three cells must be charged at a higher voltage than 6 volts. During charging a cell may rise considerably above its normal voltage, perhaps as high as 2.3 volts. If the voltage of the dynamo or other source of supply is only 6 volts there will obviously be a back pressure from the cell which may pass current through the dynamo instead of the dynamo passing current through the battery. The rate of charge of a battery should be a tenth of its actual ampère hour capacity. Never discharge a battery beyond the point where the voltage begins to fall rapidly. Never in any circumstances deliberately short circuit a battery or " spark " it, to find out whether it is charged or not. By " sparking " is meant connecting the two terminals together by a piece of wire and observing whether a spark is obtained on breaking the circuit. This is a most iniquitous practice and simply amounts to short circuiting a battery and causing a sudden and tremendous current to circulate while the battery is so short circuited. This will give rise to a tremendous disturbance of gas amounting to a miniature explosion in the substance of the plates causing the separation of portions of active material. Every cell in a battery should begin to gas at about the same time when charging. Never allow a battery to stand discharged for any length of time, always charge as soon as possible after discharge. Do not partially charge a battery. You may partially discharge it by running the set from it for an hour or two every night, but once you have started to charge it let it be completely charged before you start to discharge. When a battery is not required for some weeks take the precaution to fully charge it before putting it away. Whether a battery is being used or not it should be charged at least once every month.

HIGH TENSION BATTERIES

Our recent discussions on the subject of accumulator batteries will be associated in the mind of the reader with what is generally referred to as the "low tension battery," required to heat the filaments of the valves in the receiving apparatus. Of course, batteries of accumulators cells can be used to provide the necessary high tension voltage to the anode of the valves of the receiver. A battery of this kind generally consists of a large number of small low-capacity cells connected in series. The capacity is normally not more than 1.5 to 2 ampère hours. A battery of small capacity cells is extremely effective for this purpose, but is just as subject to the normal ailments of accumulator cells as is the low tension battery of many times the capacity, and particular care must be taken to avoid charging or discharging at rates higher than are appropriate. The difficulty of charging high tension accumulator batteries of very small capacities is to obtain a low enough rate of charging current. It is frequently the case that high tension accumulator batteries consist of blocks of 15 cells connected in series giving a E.M.F. of 30 volts. Supposing that four such blocks are used to give a voltage of 120 volts for operating the receiver, it will be best to connect the four blocks in parallel for charging purposes in order that a higher charging rate may be used than a tenth of an ampère hour capacity of each block.

The reader will remember that in our earlier studies we learnt that cells of equal capacity connected in parallel increased the total ampère hour capacity to a figure equal to the sum of the capacities of the cells so connected—that is to say, a cell having a capacity of two ampère hours connected in parallel with a similar cell would have the capacity of four ampère hours. Three cells connected in parallel would have a capacity of six ampère hours. It is obvious therefore that the rate at which the battery may be charged can be increased by connecting batteries in parallel, but it is important that the ampère hour

M

capacity of each battery connected in parallel for charging purposes should be equal because the lower the capacity of the battery the lower its internal resistance. Obviously, then, if two cells of different capacities are connected in parallel for charging purposes more current will flow through the lower capacity cell than through the other. It is the writer's experience that many listeners who use accumulator cells to provide high tension voltage for their sets are apt to neglect them, while paying scrupulous attention to the large capacity low tension filament battery. It is even more important to pay attention to each cell of a high tension accumulator battery as a unit since their construction is more delicate and consequently more subject to the ailments of accumulator batteries as discussed in previous instalments.

DRY CELLS

For the provision of the required high tension voltage for operating the valves of a receiving set dry cells are in more general use than are accumulators. The fundamental difference between a dry cell and an accumulator cell is that the former cannot in any circumstances be recharged. In point of fact, the term " dry cell " is a misnomer ; it should be properly referred to as an unspillable cell, since it relies for its action just as much on the presence of an acid solution as does the accumulator, but in a different form, as we shall see. If a term of distinction is requisite it may be referred to as a " primary " cell as opposed to the term " secondary " cell, applied to the accumulator— the distinction indicating that the former can function in one direction only, giving out energy without being able to absorb it ; while the latter can, as we know, be charged and discharged, *i.e.*, function in two opposite directions. The barest outline of the construction and action of the dry cell as it has become known is all that we need consider. Detail may be omitted because a cell or battery of cells can only be discharged once and then thrown away without hope of resuscitation. Consequently, a close study will not be of any practical assistance since the question of maintenance does not arise. The cell consists of a positive element of zinc in the form of a pot in which is the negative element of carbon surrounded by the electrolyte arranged in a semi-solid form. The solution is generally of sal-ammoniac rendered semi-solid by mixing with plaster of Paris, gelatine, or some other suitable substance. The sal-ammoniac solution is normally one part of this salt to two of water. The E.M.F. of such a cell varies between 1.4 and 1.6 volt, according to the electrolyte and elements used. A number of cells are connected in series to produce the required E.M.F., and the whole battery enclosed in a cardboard container, the space between and above each cell up to the line of the top of the container being filled with pitch or paraffin wax. The capacity of a battery of dry cells depends upon the area of positive and negative elements and upon the strength of the acid paste. It is normally very small.

When first obtained from the manufacturer the battery will be found to give a voltage slightly higher than the sum of the number of cells multiplied by 1.5. On putting it into service it will be noticed that the voltage falls rapidly to 1.5 or slightly below for each cell and should remain constant for a long time until the life of the cell begins to be exhausted. It is advisable to renew the battery as soon as the voltage falls below 1.2 per cell. A weak or failing battery is a frequent cause of bad and distorted reception because the internal resistance of a battery rises rapidly as the voltage begins to fall. Some manufacturers make what are called double capacity dry batteries, and it is as well to use these when the set is being operated at high voltages resulting in high values of anode current in the low frequency amplifying stage. In such circumstances it is really best to use H.T. accumulators. The initial cost is higher, but the life is almost illimitable if reasonable care is taken in charging and discharging.

Another disadvantage of the dry cell is that it tends to deteriorate rapidly while not in use, which the accumulator will not do if properly cared for and charged at regular intervals. On the other hand, the dry battery has the advantage of being more compact and portable and its initial cost relatively very low.

Now if the listener is fortunate enough to have a supply of electricity laid to his house, he can dispense with either type of cell and operate the set from the lighting or power mains, preferably the latter, because the cost per unit is very much less. The initial cost of the apparatus required to obtain H.T. supply from the mains is admittedly somewhat high, particularly if the current from the mains is alternating, but the cost of maintenance is practically negligible, amounting to only a few shillings a year for the current consumed.

The supply from the mains must be either direct current or alternating current. If the former, it is generally supplied from a direct current generator at the power station, and cannot be applied direct to the receiver because the commutator ripple of the generator will be present. The generator consists in principle of a coil or coils fixed in a slot cut in a soft iron core called the armature. The armature with its attached coil is rotated at a high rate between the poles of a permanent magnet. The ends of the coil are connected to segments of a circular commutator. Each segment is insulated from the next, and brushes are arranged to make contact with the segments as they rotate. Obviously, as the coil rotates between the poles of the magnet the polarity of its two ends will be reversed with every half revolution of the armature. By having two brushes 180 degrees apart making contact with the segments, one brush must be picking up a positive voltage while the other is picking up a negative one. Thus the current in a circuit having its two ends connected one to each brush is a unidirectional current, *but* the current is not steady because the coils are changing polarity through zero, and consequently the voltage must rise and fall with each half revolution. This will produce a rippling sound in the set if the mains, the terminal points of which are connected to the brushes of the generator at the power station, are connected directly to the set. The frequency of the ripple will obviously be proportional to the speed at which the armature of the generator is rotated. To get rid of this ripple we must use what is called a smoothing or filter circuit. This circuit consists of a combination of capacity and inductance.

We know from our earlier studies that the resistance of a condenser varies according to the frequency of any alternating or fluctuating current which it may be required to pass. To put it another way, we may say that a condenser is capable of choosing between high and low fre-

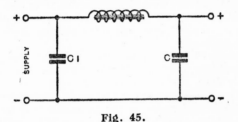

Fig. 45.

quencies according to its capacity. The lower the frequency of the ripple, the greater must be the capacity of the condenser, because its resistance to a frequency of, say, 50 cycles gets lower and lower as its capacity is increased. For the mathematically-minded reader we may break the rule against formulæ which we made at the beginning of this series, and give the following very simple one. The resistance to the flow of an alternating current which will be afforded by a condenser is expressed by $\frac{1}{2} \pi$ f.c. when π is 3.14159, F is the frequency of alternation of the supply and c is the capacity of the condenser in microfarads. Supposing that the ripple we want to filter has a frequency of 50 cycles, let the reader who is sufficiently interested work out the resistance of a condenser of .001 microfarad and of another of 8 microfarads and observe the difference. The resistance of the latter is almost negligible. If, then, we connect a large condenser across the mains and earth one side of them, we are providing an easy path to earth for the unwanted voltage variation, and the result will be to smooth the supply.

But this is not enough in itself for practical purposes. We must also connect an inductance in *series* with one or both leads from the mains. The inductance has to deal with a very low frequency, and we want it to afford the maximum possible resistance to the unwanted frequency. It must therefore have a very high value of inductance, and generally takes the form of an iron cored choked coil. The most usual arrangement of a complete filter unit is that shown diagrammatically in Fig 45. It is of little use to describe the values of the choke and condensers, since these will vary with the frequency of the supply ripple. For a rough guide, however, and as many mains have a frequency of about 50 cycles, it may be stated that a choke having an inductance of some 50 henries and condensers of 4 microfarads each will be satisfactory. Before install-ing apparatus to provide H.T. from D.C. mains it is as well to ascertain which side of the supply is earthed. If the positive side is earthed, the supply company should be approached and requested to change over. To discover the polarity of the mains, attach one wire to each terminal and hold the ends of the two wires in a glass of water. The wire which gives off bubbles is attached to the negative terminal.

A friend has asked whether it is possible to heat the filaments of the valves from the D.C. mains. It is possible, but the writer does not recommend the practice because it is very much more difficult to eliminate all traces of ripple if both the filament and anode currents are supplied from the mains. It is a simpler and generally a better practice to use a low tension battery to supply the filament current. This battery can be charged quite easily and conveniently from the D.C. mains. All that is necessary is to insert resistances between one of the mains terminals and the battery in order to reduce the voltage of the mains to a value which is suitable for the purpose. Carbon filament lamps will be found suitable

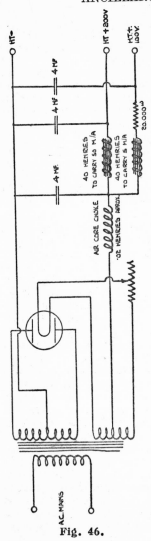

Fig. 46.

for this purpose. The application of Ohm's law (current is equal to voltage divided by resistance) will at once indicate the number and type of lamps or value of any other resistances which may be required to charge a battery of any particular voltage at its appropriate charging rate. No smoothing apparatus is necessary since current is unidirectional and the ripple is of no consequence provided that the battery is not used to light the valves of the receiving set at the same time as it is being charged. To revert to the supply of anode current from D.C. mains, it will be found in many cases that the supply is at too high a voltage even after smoothing where a certain voltage drop is bound to occur due to the resistance of the choke coil and smoothing condensers. The voltage will not be too high for the amplifier valves if these are of the proper type, but it may easily be higher than is needed for the rectifier valve and may render the set unstable and prone to oscillation. Particularly is this the case where the coupling between the rectifier valve and the first low frequency amplifier valve consists of a transformer or a choke and not a resistance. The voltage can be reduced by inserting a resistance between the positive terminal of the smoothing unit and the rectifier valve anode. It is of the greatest importance to ensure the complete absence of ripple in the supply to the anode of the rectifier valve, and for this reason it is often as well to insert an additional condenser across the rectifier supply. So much for H.T. from D.C. mains.

H.T. FROM A.C. MAINS

Now let us consider the means by which H.T. may be derived from A.C. mains. The listener whose house is supplied with alternating current has one very distinct advantage over the less fortunate consumer of direct current, in that the former can make his voltage what he wants by the use of a transformer, whereas the latter is restricted as to maximum by the voltage of the mains less any drop which may occur in the smoothing unit. This point is of particular importance where high voltages are required to operate an amplifier of considerable power. The reader will recollect from earlier discussions that the alternating voltage induced in the secondary of a transformer has a value in relation to the voltage of the primary, which is approximately proportional to the ratio of turns constituting the primary and secondary windings. That is to say, if the alternating voltage from the mains is 200 volts and the two ends of the primary of a transformer are connected to the mains terminals the voltage of the secondary will be 400 volts, if the number of turns of wire on the secondary is twice that of the primary, or 600 volts, if it is three times. The supply must be rectified or converted from alternating to unidirectional current. For this purpose we require two-electrode valves. Several makes of two-electrode valves specially designed for the purpose are produced by manufacturers, and it is as well to use one of these types, although a three-electrode valve can be used quite satisfactorily and converted into a three-electrode valve by strapping the grid and anode connection of the valve holder with a short length of wire. The action of a two-electrode valve as a rectifier has already been discussed fully in an earlier instalment (page 61), to illustrate the elementary principles governing the operation of the valve as an accessory to radio communication. Nothing need be added to this previous discussion or to the illustrations which accompanied it, except to say that it is more usual in practice to heat the filaments of the two-electrode valves by alternating current fed through a separate secondary winding on the transformer, thus dispensing with the battery. It may be mentioned that it is not always necessary to use two separate valves to provide full wave rectification. Some manufacturers produce specially designed valves having two anodes. The effect and operation are exactly the same. It is in effect two valves accommodated in one vacuum tube. The rectified output will be unidirectional, but will not be completely steady, even though double wave rectification is used. There is bound to be fluctuation which would result in a humming sound having a frequency equal to that of the alternations of the supply if the rectified output were applied directly to the receiver. A smoothing unit must be used which may be similar in construction and operation to that which is used to smooth the ripple from D.C. mains, but the values of the components will vary according to the frequency of alternation of the supply. Fig. 46 shows a complete rectifying and smoothing circuit using a double anode valve, together with tappings arranged to provide lower voltage to the rectifier valve.